MONSTER SPOTTER'S
Guide to North America

SCOTT FRANCIS
with illustrations by Ben Patrick

HOW BOOKS Cincinnati, Ohio
www.howdesign.com

For more fine books from F+W Publications, visit www.fw-
bookstore.com.

11 10 09 08 07   5 4 3 2 1

Distributed in Canada by Fraser Direct, 100 Armstrong Avenue,
Georgetown, Ontario, Canada L7G 5S4, Tel: (905) 877-4411.
Distributed in the U.K. and Europe by David & Charles, Brunel
House, Newton Abbot, Devon, TQ12 4PU, England, Tel: (+44)
1626 323200, Fax: (+44) 1626 323319, E-mail: postmaster@davi-
dandcharles.co.uk. Distributed in Australia by Capricorn Link, P.O.
Box 704, Windsor, NSW 2756 Australia, Tel: (02) 4577-3555.

Library of Congress Cataloging-in-Publication Data

Francis, Scott.
  The monster spotter's guide to North America / by Scott
Francis. -- 1st ed.
      p. cm.
  Includes bibliographical references and index.
  ISBN-13: 978-1-58180-929-9 (pbk. : alk. paper)
  ISBN-10: 1-58180-929-8
  1. Monsters--North America. 2. North America--Folklore.
I. Title.
  GR825.F73 2007
  398.24'54--dc22   2007008512

Edited by Amy Schell
Designed by Grace Ring
Illustrations by Ben Patrick
Production coordinated by Greg Nock

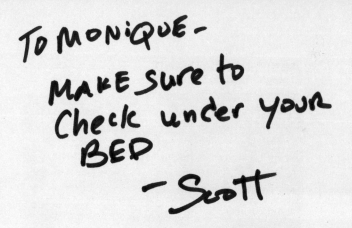

To MONIQUE—

MAKE sure to Check under your BED

— Scott

"Don't write this book. You'll perform a disservice to a field of inquiry that has always struggled for respectability."

—**Special Agent Fox Mulder***

The X-Files, Season 3, "Jose Chung's 'From Outer Space'"

About the Illustrator

A native Ohioan, Benjamin E. Patrick is a professional designer, illustrator, and conspiracy theorist. He cites an encounter with a Loveland Frog Man as an early influence on his artistic and mental development. He lives with his lovely wife and some yet-to-be-categorized cryptids.

About the Author

Photo courtesy of Heather Francis.

Aside from being a monster enthusiast, Scott Francis is a founding editor for the literary journal *Fresh Boiled Peanuts* and coauthor of *The Writer's Book of Matches*. He holds a black belt in Tae Kwon Do and lives his life according to a strict moral code of his own devising. A native of the mountainous regions of North Carolina, he currently lives in Cincinnati with his very patient and understanding wife, three cats, and a sinister black dog of possible supernatural origin.

Acknowledgments

I'd like to thank my family, friends and co-workers who listened to countless monster stories and managed to always seem genuinely interested. Many of you inspired me along the way, and I'd like to dedicate specific monsters to some of you: the Kushtaka to Becky, the Fouke Monster to Paul, the Iliamna Lake Monsters to my mom, the Snipe to my Pap-paw, the Flitterbick to Peggy, El Vampiro de Moca to my fellow *FBP* staff members, the Mothman to the entire M-Day crew, the Mulberry Black Thing to Brooke, the Lake Leelanau Monster to Glen and Lisa, the Gatormen to Cheryl and Jim, the Manitou to Greg, the Loveland Frogman to my editor Amy, the Sasquatch to Matt and Barb, the Jackalope to Steve, the Black Dog of West Peak to Grace, the Jersey Devil to Phil, the polar-grizzlies to Shawn, El Chupacabra to Greg in production, the bizarre mutant dog carcass from Maine to Karen and to Ben and Megan, and the Sidehill Wampus to my father.

The writing of this book has been an arduous task and one that I couldn't have completed without the support of my very patient and understanding wife, Heather. She took photos on our excursions, listened to me read excerpts aloud and sacrificed her time to patiently pretend to read magazines while asleep on the couch whenever I was writing. To her, I dedicate the Devil Monkey.

TABLE OF CONTENTS

Introduction

Why Monsters?

Since early man began to walk upright, stopped dragging his knuckles, and figured out how to draw pictures on a cave wall with a burnt stick, animal blood, and some juice from mashed-up berries or whatever, humans have recorded encounters with weird, often frightening creatures. Every civilization has its monster myths—consider the Egyptian Sphinx, the Chinese Dragon and the Basilisk of European folklore, to name just a few.

When the Europeans came to North America, they found a new world rich in its own myth and folklore. Native Americans told of a whole slew of fantastic and horrifying beings from lake serpents and gargantuan birds to strange woodland dwarves and giants. The native folklore was in the very least as colorful as the mythology of the Greeks and the Romans. The Americas spread forth before Europeans—a wild pagan land full of mystery and opportunities just ripe for exploiting. And exploit they did. Forests were razed and species were molested or wiped out. Native people were conquered and their traditions were portrayed as evil, making way for Christianity. The strange animals of their legends became devils. Their enchanted forests became realms of dark, forbidden magic.

And no one could stay away. The more forbidden the stories were, the more of a grasp they took on our folklore. Monsters and ghosts became entertainment—tales to be whispered by a campfire. Lumberjacks and prospectors blamed their misfortunes on unseen beasts that wreaked havoc and played mischief in the night.

Monsters have always had a hold on our imaginations. There's something primal about monster stories. They're scary, of course, but it's more than that. They're always somehow familiar.

I remember as a kid the nostalgic feeling that would creep over me when I heard my father begin to tell of the Wampus Cats rumored to stalk the hills of Appalachia. "Oh, the Wampus—it's a fearsome critter ... " he would begin. Was I scared? Of course. Did I want to be scared? Absolutely.

The Wampus of my father's childhood haunted the small town where he grew up. The neighbors told of frightening yowls in the night and the banging of upset garbage cans. The beast held them captive. During the course of a summer, no one dared venture out after dark for fear of the dreaded Wampus. The same creature haunted my own childhood. It was one of the stories my father told on hot summer nights when sitting on the front porch with my mother and their grownup friends. There were other stories, such as the mysterious Brown Mountain Lights of Burke County, North Carolina—according to some legends, they are caused by the ghostly lantern of a long-dead slave searching for his master; others believe the lights are actually flying saucers. I was enthralled by such stories. And I'm pretty sure I'm not alone.

Since I started writing this book, I have been given monster tips from friends, family and coworkers about a local legend from when they were growing up, or some bizarre creature sighting they read about in the news. During the course of this writing, there were sightings of the lake monster known as Champ, a bizarre mutant dog carcass was found in Maine, and the body of a creepy-looking mermaid washed up on a beach in Venda, South Africa. I was sent all kinds of weird stuff, from an urban legend about an ethereal black entity capable of assuming any form, to theories about the origins of Jackalopes. People stopped me in the halls to tell me about strange hybrid bears that were discovered in the Arctic—an apparent cross between a polar bear and a grizzly. I've discussed coelacanths with folks at work. I was even approached with actual photographic evidence of an alleged Sasquatch, which I'll share with you later in this book.

Whether you are fascinated or terrified, monsters are almost impossible to ignore. They represent the dark side of humanity—the primal, animal impulses (greed, hunger, lust) that reside in every single one of us beneath the tamed, educated and socially conditioned personalities we put forth. In some cases, monsters may end up being strange and wonderful animals that have somehow remained hidden from the watchful eye of modern science. Philosophical or scientific, the reasons why monsters have such a hold on our culture are real.

I have always loved monsters and ghost stories. My favorite children's books told of fantastic beasts, mermaids and other weird creatures—how could you not love Maurice Sendak's *Where the Wild Things Are*? Halloween was (and still is) the best holiday—filled with an air of mystery and nostalgia. Like many in their early teens, I devoured horror movies. I tended to be more enamored of the ones featuring vampires, werewolves and other monsters than the psycho-killer flicks. If I was walking through our neighborhood alone in the dark, I would often imagine some unseen evil entity just behind me. My fear would mount until I could no longer will myself to continue my normal pace, and I'd break into a full run until I reached home. At night in bed, I would cover my head with the sheets as I imagined terrible creatures lurking in my closet and sneaking around my room. It was equal parts fear and entertainment.

Some years later, I learned from my father that it is possible to replicate the terrifying guttural cry of the female Wampus using a tin can and a string coated in beeswax. What possible use could a youth living in a small Appalachian town have for such a device? I'm pretty sure he was out hunting monsters.

The Perils of Monster Hunting

Monster hunting is a dangerous avocation. Do you have a television? Have you ever watched *Buffy the Vampire Slayer*? Were you living a cave during the nine seasons that *The X-Files* was airing? Someone always dies. Monsters kill people—at least most of them do, anyway. It's not their fault, really ... it's just what monsters do. Call it a character flaw. It's like sharks. Are you surprised when you hear about some surfer in Recife, Brazil, who gets his leg bitten off?

As a monster hunter, you might find yourself out in the woods armed with a rifle loaded with silver bullets. Your friends might already have been dragged off into the woods to be eaten. That is, if you have any friends in the first place; when you go around raving about monsters, people tend not to talk to you. But I digress. You're in the woods with no friends. You try to keep your wits about you. You step lightly, rifle at the ready. A twig snaps behind you and you freeze. You spin round, taking aim at ... nothing. From behind you comes a low growl and you whirl around and fire your weapon into thin air. Again and again, there is nothing there, until you realize you've wasted your last silver bullet. You find yourself running through the woods in a blind panic. Branches slap you in the face and you stumble over fallen trees until you finally turn your ankle on a loose rock. You collapse on your leg with your full body weight, wrenching the tendons and tearing the muscles in your calf. You gasp in pain and struggle to roll over, looking up to see the inevitable...

And even if you don't find yourself being devoured by the missing link in the middle of the woods, there are plenty of other dangers. You could get lost and find yourself wandering around the forest in circles until you succumb to the elements and some hiker finds your skeletal remains in the mud. You could be mistaken for a quail and shot by a shotgun-toting redneck. You could end up in some sort of Jon Voigt-esque scenario where you find yourself being hunted by a banjo-playing backwoods local who makes pig noises. You could be bitten by a snake, be mauled by a bear or simply fall off a cliff. Just about anything can happen. Nature doesn't care about you. There's a bunch more where you came from, and besides, your kind keeps chopping down her trees anyway.

All physical peril aside, consider the embarrassment. Let's say you go out and shoot yourself a real-life monster. You have it preserved as evidence to show to the world. Next thing you know, your friends are saying it's a fake. That you had a taxidermist attach antlers to the head of an ordinary rabbit and that it doesn't even look that real anyway. You're a laughingstock—a footnote in a bar story.

Monsters are illusory—another one of their character flaws. Chasing after evidence of them can cost you more than your life. You could lose your livelihood, your spouse, your friends, your credibility, your sobriety and your sanity. So where does that leave you?

Like me, maybe you really like monsters. You watch Buffy and her friends go out and dust themselves a vampire, or cage a werewolf, and you think about going to your job the next day and it really, really sucks. You wonder why you can't live your dream and chase after monsters. You don't even care that much if you get superpowers or not—you could just work out a lot and train to be proficient with weapons. Then you remember that monster hunting doesn't pay and that just yesterday you dropped fifty bones at the comic book store.

As you can see, being a monster enthusiast can be a slippery slope. Like anything, if you let your passion for monsters get the better of you, you might find yourself without a job and, to put it bluntly, without a life. So, yeah—you should probably go to work. And maybe don't mention the monsters while you're there.

But take heart. You don't have to give up your dreams. It's possible to lead a normal life and still enjoy the search for the unexplained—that's exactly what this book is all about.

How to Become a Monster Spotter

Monster spotting is a much healthier alternative to monster hunting. I like to think of it as the paranormal equivalent to bird-watching. It's possible to engage in your monster research as a hobby. Not only can you lead a normal life while pursuing your paranormal interests on the side, but you'll also be able to simply shrug when someone makes fun of you. Just say something like, "Doesn't everyone have weird hobbies?" Some people might even find it endearing. Think of the freedom.

Plus, imagine actually having something to do on those uneventful vacations. Instead of sitting around a beach or in a hotel trying to pick a restaurant, or bickering about which tourist trap to visit next, you could be out enjoying nature and learning about local history—all while searching for monsters. Vacationers often lack direction and end up feeling like they are wasting their precious time off. Monster spotting can unite the unmotivated and give them a sense of purpose and direction. Your family and friends will love it.

Being a monster spotter can be as easy as it is rewarding. Before setting out on a vacation or a weekend trip, do a quick Internet search for local monster legends. It's pretty much as easy as using your favorite web browser and typing in the area name and "monsters." If you don't have any luck, try using some other words—"myths," "folklore" … stuff like that. You're sure to find lots of Native American lore that may have ties to modern monster legends. Remember, even if particular towns do not have a monster legend, chances are the surrounding areas do.

It's also important to keep an open mind when monster spotting. I've found that when I'm doing monster research or am on the trail of a particular legend, I'll run across something of equal or greater interest. Looking for monsters is kind of like looking for a set of lost keys. Maybe you have good reason to believe you lost your keys in the couch. You start moving the cushions and rummaging around. You may or may not find your keys, but if your couch is anything like mine, chances are you'll find something—a Yoda action figure, $3.76 in coins, the retainer you wore in junior high … something. The possibilities are limitless. And that's exactly my point. When you start looking, you never know what you might find. As a monster spotter, it's important to remember that *what* you are searching for is not as important as the fact that you are indeed searching.

Types of Monsters

Monsters often defy description. They can vary in size and shape. Their footprints can have differing numbers of toes. They may have different colors of fur, or have scales, or be slick and slimy. It's hard to know exactly how monsters are related to each other in the monster world because so much of what we know about them depends upon secondhand information. Facts become warped through elaboration and embellishment. Like fish in tales told by aging anglers, monsters get larger every time the story is told. Their eyes take on a red glow instead of simply being a flash in the headlights.

The very folklorish aspects that make monster stories so much fun also make it difficult to draw clear connections between seemingly related phenomena and lump them into categories. It's been done numerous times and in ways that make sense, but there are always monsters that don't quite seem to fit or have traits that could fit in with another group. Nevertheless, what follows is an overview of the typical classifications that monsters fit into ... more or less.

Sasquatch and Hairy Monsters

Bigfoot. It's the most recognized monster name in America, probably in the world. The term has been used all across the country to describe legends of hairy monsters. To the uninformed, any hairy monster could be a Bigfoot. When you dig deeper, you learn more details that separate Bigfoot from other hairy monsters reported across the continent. There are differences in size, number of toes, color of fur and markings, behavior and appetites. North America seems to be home to a few—possibly related—species of primate-like creatures that tend to inhabit particular regions. Some, such as the Sasquatch of the Pacific Northwest and Canada, are often portrayed as gentle lumbering giants who shyly forage for berries and other vegetation in the woods. Others, such as the Skunk Apes of the South, can be very aggressive and should be considered a danger to pets, livestock and possibly even humans.

Reports of hairy apelike monsters are so numerous throughout North America that it is very difficult to totally dismiss the possibility of their existence. Many scientists, even skeptical ones, have dedicated a good deal of time to researching Bigfoot reports and examining the evidence that has been collected throughout the years.

Flying Monsters

Unlike Bigfoot-type monsters, which usually have a fairly universal appearance, flying monsters have been reported in a wide array of varying descriptions. Giant birds resembling the Thunderbird of Native American legends have been seen from the Southwest to the Midwest, often appearing as large condor-like birds with twenty-foot wingspans. Other Thunderbird accounts describe even stranger creatures looking more reptilian than avian, and bearing an uncanny resemblance to flying dinosaurs such as pterodactyls. Even stranger still are accounts of birdlike creatures that glide without flapping their wings, such as the Texas winged monster known as Big Bird.

Throughout the years, people have seen all manner of weird things in the sky, from winged griffin-like animals to flying men with bat wings, such as the one spotted over New York's Coney Island in the late 1800s. Children have been snatched up by the talons of giant birds and lifted off the ground. Ghostly lights have been seen moving through the night sky. Many believe that flying beasts patrol the sky and swoop down on livestock in the middle of the night, leaving behind mutilated or blood-drained corpses.

Whatever form they take, flying monsters are some of the most frightening and vicious of the creatures included in this book. I urge you to use caution when searching for such beasts and to always keep an eye to the skies.

Ocean, Lake and River Monsters

When I told friends I was writing a book about monsters, most of them would raise an eyebrow and say, "You mean like Loch Ness Monsters?" I would in turn carefully explain that not all lake monsters should be called Loch Ness Monsters, that Nessie is an individual and actually not a subject I would tackle in depth because she inhabits Loch Ness in Scotland and my book is about monsters indigenous to North America, but that many of the monsters in my book do indeed live in lakes and may be related to her.

Most of my friends were either annoyed or amused by my long-winded pseudo-intellectual response but seemed to remain interested—and for good reason. Aquatic monsters are fascinating. They represent some of the most credible encounters with monster phenomena. When looking into a large body of water, it is easy to imagine some large creature lurking in the cold, dark depths. When you consider the descriptions of most lake and sea monsters, you find that most of them resemble prehistoric creatures that actually existed. Coupled with the fact that freakish-looking fish still inhabit the depths of the oceans, including some that were once thought to be extinct, such as the coelacanth, it doesn't seem like such a stretch to believe that some snaky eel-like thing might be swimming in those murky depths.

So how can you write a monster book and not cover Nessie, the most famous aquatic enigma of all time? The answer is that you really can't. But you should know that this great continent of ours has plenty of amazing lake monsters of its very own. Really. In fact, Canada's lakes are practically teeming with monsters. There happen to be more than ten documented lake serpents in her waters. Ogopogo, the serpent of Canada's Lake Okanagan, was first sighted nearly sixty years before the first reports of the Loch Ness Monster. Champ's home of Lake Champlain, while not as deep as Loch Ness, is much larger (Loch Ness covers approximately 22 square miles to Lake Champlain's roughly 430 square miles). Still hung up on the Loch Ness Monster? Well, you might find this interesting: Loch Ness, Lake Okanagan and Lake Champlain are similar in depth and water temperature, and all lie at nearly the same latitude (in fact, there are over fifteen lake monsters reported between the forty-fifth and fiftieth parallels). What does that tell you? Most lake monsters like cold, deep water. Now you know where to look ... or where not to swim. (Not that you would anyway—it's cold).

Folklore Monsters

Perhaps the most fun monsters of all are the monsters of American folklore. Often referred to as "fearsome critters," these wild beasts were blamed for accidents and mischief by lumberjacks and other settlers. Often oddly shaped with wild attributes, these creatures are uniquely American. From exploding bears to beasts with telescoping legs for navigating rocky mountainsides, the monsters of American folklore are usually strange hybrids of different animals. Some are frightening, but most are simply bizarre and occasionally hilarious.

UFO-Related Monsters

I hate to admit it, but aliens probably get more exposure than monsters. Don't get me wrong; as a paranormal enthusiast I find greys (see glossary for definition) as creepy and cool as the next guy, but I hate to see them steal the show. Luckily for me, there's a lot of crossover. Flying monsters are by their very definition unidentified flying objects, or UFOs, and are often speculated to be extraterrestrial in nature. Weirdly, many Bigfoot sightings coincide with reports of flying saucers. Descriptions of El Chupacabra, with its skinny forearms and large oval eyes, greatly resemble those of your typical grey alien. Some Native American legends tell of small, spindly limbed dwarfs, such as the Mannegishi, which lived in the forest—creatures that sound eerily like the archetypal space alien.

Reptilian Humanoids

This particular class of monsters represents where the lines between categories of monsters blur, and things get a little confusing. Details and circumstances surrounding reports of reptilian humanoids often sound quite similar to your typical

Bigfoot-esque hairy monster sighting, but their lizard or frog-like visages often conjure up a logical connection to lake and river monsters. Like hairy monsters, reptilian humanoids seem to have a tendency to wander roads and approach (sometimes attack) automobiles. They are often (but not always) spotted near bodies of water. To make things even more convoluted, there are cases of extraterrestrial beings that are reported as having a reptilian appearance. Are these strange beings indeed connected to UFO phenomena, or are they amphibious beings that occasionally emerge from bodies of water to wander the forests, where they are mistaken for a Bigfoot?

Phantom Animals

Ever heard the one about alligators in the sewers? Urban legends about displaced animals turning up in weird places are so abundant they have almost lost their shock value. Throughout modern history, folks have reported sightings of animals in areas where they clearly do not belong.

Large mystery cats have been reported throughout Appalachia and the Midwest—places mountain lions do not typically inhabit. In many cases, these cats are described as resembling black panthers, which is definitely strange, since black panthers are not supposed to be indigenous to North America.

In the Midwest there have been numerous reports of kangaroo sightings. People have reported them jumping across the road in front of cars, hopping through cornfields and skulking around homes. They've even been seen in urban areas, including Chicago. As if that isn't strange enough, these phantom kangaroos are often portrayed as incredibly aggressive and abnormal, seemingly possessing strange claws and fangs.

So maybe you're thinking, "Okay, these animal sightings are weird, but can we really call them monsters?" That's a valid question, but imagine if we actually find out that black panthers or kangaroos are indeed indigenous to North America, and they have simply been incredibly wily and have managed to avoid humans all this time. Wouldn't that open the door for other fringe possibilities? Bigfoot could have done the same thing, and if Bigfoot is real, what about El Chupacabra, and so forth? Once you cross the line to considering that a monster legend like Bigfoot might actually be attributed to sightings of an undiscovered and misunderstood animal, it's not too much of a leap to look at other monsters with an open mind.

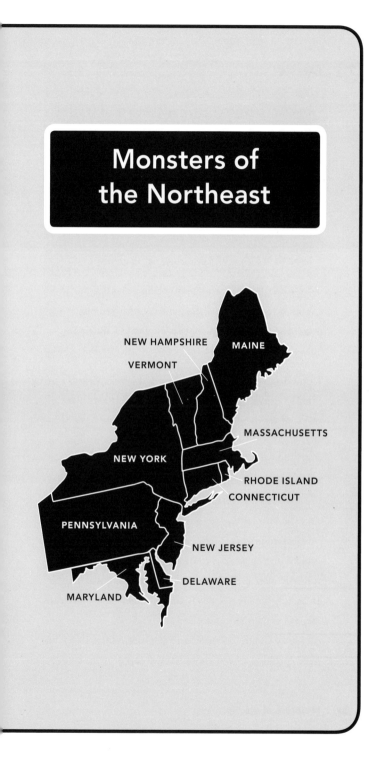

Monsters of
the Northeast

NEW HAMPSHIRE

MAINE

VERMONT

MASSACHUSETTS

NEW YORK

RHODE ISLAND

CONNECTICUT

PENNSYLVANIA

NEW JERSEY

DELAWARE

MARYLAND

⟨🐍⟩ Bessie

CHARACTERISTICS: Gray snakelike body; in some reports, it has "arms"

SIZE: Most probably thirty to forty feet in length with a body approximately one foot in diameter, although there are some reports of a much larger beast

HABITAT: Lake Erie

APPETITE: Fish and the occasional swimmer

PRECAUTIONS: I recommend using at least a thirty-pound test line and a sturdy rod … and you may want to think twice about swimming in Lake Erie.

Known as South Bay Bessie, the Lake Erie Monster or simply Bessie, this creature has been the subject of monster sightings since the late 1800s. There have been many false reports surrounding the Bessie phenomena, including a case where two men claimed to have clubbed a "sea serpent" and captured it. It was later discovered that the men worked for a touring carnival and the animal was actually an unfortunate python.

Despite practical jokes and hoaxes, Bessie sightings and swimmer attacks persist. There is even a rumor of a Bessie attack that claimed the lives of three people in which the creature was described as having a head larger than an automobile.

Many Bessie reports have been attributed to sturgeon, prehistoric-looking fish that can grow to be over one hundred years old, exceed seven feet in length and weigh more than three hundred pounds.

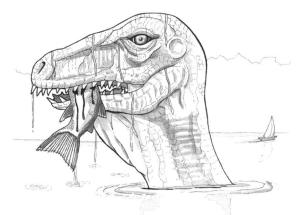

The Black Dog of West Peak

CHARACTERISTICS: As the name suggests, this apparition appears to be a black canine, usually described as a small, friendly spaniel with sad eyes.

SIZE: About two feet in length—a moderately sized dog

HABITAT: The West Peak of the Hanging Hills of Meriden, Connecticut

APPETITE: Believed to be a ghost, the Black Dog probably has no need for food

PRECAUTIONS: The Black Dog is thought to be a bad omen—if you see this creature once, it is recommended that you never return to the Hanging Hills.

Home to sites named Misery Brook, Lamentation Mountain and Black Pond, Connecticut's Hanging Hills of Meriden is an area enveloped in mystery and legend. The mountains were created from ancient lava flows, giving them plenty of unusual rock formations and craggy outcroppings that make them interesting sites for exploration and more than a little bit creepy. The area is an obvious draw for mountain climbers, hikers and nature lovers as well as geologists. The mountain paths are challenging and can be hazardous even in the best of conditions.

The area's West Peak, which rises approximately three thousand feet above sea level, is the home of a scary legend known as the Black Dog of West Peak. The dog is thought to be a ghost of some sort and is an omen of bad things to come. The apparition appears as a small, friendly dog with sad eyes and seems normal in all respects, until it barks or howls without making a sound.

The dog will disappear, leaving no footprints or trace of its existence. Legend has it that "if a man shall meet the Black Dog once, it shall be for joy; and if twice, it shall be for sorrow; and the third time, he shall die."[1]

The most notable account of encounters with the Black Dog of West Peak was made in the late 1800s by geologist W.H.C. Pynchon, who described meeting the dog while on a trip to the West Peak to collect samples of lava rocks. Pynchon described a friendly, small black dog that accompanied him through the course of the day only to later vanish inexplicably. Three years later, he returned to the site with his friend and fellow geologist Herbert Marshall, who confessed to having seen the dog twice before and laughed at the legend. The next day the pair again saw the apparition just before Marshall slipped on some loose rock and fell to his death. Grief stricken, Pynchon felt compelled to return to the area to continue the geological survey despite the legend. Six years later he returned to the West Peak, and his body was found in nearly the exact location as that of his friend's.

The Black Dog of West Peak is still seen on occasion in the Hanging Hills area and continues to be blamed for "accidental" deaths that occur in the mountains. The legend has much in common with worldwide reports of spectral black dogs that are seen as portents of impending death.

See also *Black Dogs*, page 188.

---

1 This quote is a local saying, as retold by geologist W.H.C. Pynchon in his firsthand account of meeting The Black Dog of West Peak (published in *The Connecticut Quarterly* in 1898).

The Black Fox of Salmon River

CHARACTERISTICS: Luxurious black fur

SIZE: Fox-sized

HABITAT: The wooded areas surrounding the Salmon River, Connecticut

APPETITE: Likely small woodland animals, such as squirrels and rabbits

PRECAUTIONS: Possesses the ability to enchant humans, luring them into the depths of the forest.

This ghostly animal is said to have inhabited the shores of Connecticut's Salmon River since before European settlers came to the area. Native Americans told of a beautiful black fox with a thick, shiny pelt that could not be killed or captured. Indian braves coveted the

animal's beautiful hide, but their arrows could never seem to find their mark. Hunters would chase the animal into the woods only to return days later exhausted and empty-handed.

Settlers began to see the animal, too, and hunters and trappers have been lured deep into the woods, where many became lost and most likely died from exhaustion and exposure. Legend has it that the urge to chase the Black Fox is overwhelming and anyone who sees it will be filled with an inexplicable desire to possess its beautiful coat.

The Black River Monster

CHARACTERISTICS: Dark-colored serpentine body with large bulging eyes

---

SIZE: Approximately twenty feet long

HABITAT: New York's Black River

APPETITE: Unknown

PRECAUTIONS: Creature is known to appear during electrical storms, and every precaution should be made to protect yourself and any electrical equipment from the weather.

First reported in 1951, this strange creature is only seen a few times every decade. Its description matches that of typical aquatic monster lore, with its snakelike appearance (and occasionally mentioned flippers). The beast seems to be linked in some way to electrical storms, which is the only time it tends to show itself.

(ℜ) Champ

CHARACTERISTICS: Slimy gray skin, a snakelike body and a horselike head

---

SIZE: Approximately twenty to thirty feet in length

HABITAT: Lake Champlain, which occupies parts of New York, Vermont and Quebec

---

APPETITE: Most likely fish

PRECAUTIONS: Champ is a protected animal. Aside from getting injured, you should know that any harmful contact you initiate with an undiscovered species fitting Champ's description in the Lake Champlain vicinity might incur legal ramifications.

Champ is the almost affectionate name given to a creature (or group of creatures) thought to live in Lake Champlain, which is the largest lake in America next to the Great Lakes at roughly one hundred miles in length, thirteen miles in width and a maximum depth of four hundred feet. Put simply, Champ is the Loch Ness Monster of the United States. (If you're unfamiliar with the Loch Ness Monster, please visit Appendix A, page 208.)

The Champ phenomenon boasts some of the most dramatic and credible sightings in the history of cryptozoology. Sightings of this monster have been documented even before Europeans began exploration in North America. Native American legends describe animals that fit the description, which they called *Chaousarou*—later described by explorer Samuel de Champlain as a twenty-foot-long, serpentine creature.

During the late 1800s, there were a whole slew of Champ sightings, eventually leading showman P.T. Barnum to offer a reward of fifty thousand dollars for the beast's carcass so he might add it to a traveling exhibit. The sightings continued as Champ seemed fond of surfacing alongside yacht and canoe outings, occasionally getting stuck in shallow water, allowing shocked onlookers a chance to watch for several minutes before escaping to return to the depths.

The drama came to a climax in 1977 when a woman named Sandra Mansi and her family were enjoying an afternoon on the Vermont side of the lake when she saw Champ's neck surface from the lake. She watched in horror as the creature's neck swayed in a snake-like fashion as it surveyed the shoreline, but gathered her wits and ran to the car to grab her camera. The resulting photograph is one of the most convincing pieces of monster evidence ever recorded. Despite numerous examinations, the photo has never been proven a hoax.

Scientific interest generated by the sightings—particularly the efforts of the Lake Champlain Phenomena Investigation organized by cryptozoologist Joseph Zarzynski—led to the passing of legislation in both Vermont and New York that protects Champ from any willful harm.

Investigators believe Champ to be a sort of prehistoric throwback. There is speculation that the animal is in fact a plesiosaur (a marine reptile thought to be extinct) or possibly a zeuglodon (a type of primitive whale also considered extinct).

Chessie

CHARACTERISTICS: Dark-colored snakelike body with flippers

SIZE: Approximately thirty feet long

HABITAT: Chesapeake Bay

APPETITE: Fish, most likely

PRECAUTIONS: Chessie is reported to be playful and is not typically feared by bay residents.

Like many aquatic monsters, the Chesapeake Bay Monster, more affectionately known as Chessie, is believed by many to be a prehistoric creature. Sightings typically describe the creature swimming through the bay with "humps" protruding from the water. There are no reports that link the monster to any aggressive behavior, and it has even been known to try to play with swimmers by diving beneath the water to surface on the other side of them.

Interestingly, in 1994 a manatee was captured in the Chesapeake Bay and returned to its native Florida waters.

Coonigators

CHARACTERISTICS: Rounded bodies with gray fur and reptilian faces

SIZE: Roughly the same size as a raccoon

HABITAT: Wooded areas surrounding Montpelier, Vermont

APPETITE: These animals are scavengers and are reported to raid trash cans and campground dumpsters.

PRECAUTIONS: Like alligators, these creatures are said to have a mouth full of dangerous, sharp teeth.

Not much is known about these strange animals. According to reports, they look like something out of the movie *Critters*, resembling raccoons in both appearance and behavior, except that they have fearsome alligator-like faces. If camping in the Montpelier area, it is advisable to maintain a clean campsite, disposing of food remnants and garbage quickly and thoroughly.

The Dover Demon

CHARACTERISTICS: Tan-colored skin, a large bulbous head with big reflective eyes that may appear green or bright orange; skinny neck and body with spindly limbs and long narrow digits

---

SIZE: Approximately three feet tall

HABITAT: Wooded areas of Dover, Massachusetts, near the Charles River

---

APPETITE: Unknown

PRECAUTIONS: Encounters with this creature have been brief, leaving its behavioral patterns undetermined. One should use extreme caution approaching this beast, as with any unpredictable animal.

The Dover Demon is the name given to a creature involved in a particular case that occurred in April of 1977. Several teenagers in three separate incidents occurring over five days spotted the creature. The incident received quite a bit of media coverage and led to a great deal of speculation. All of the witnesses were considered by local authorities and numerous reporters to be credible (although one of them confessed to smoking marijuana prior to the sighting).

Drawings by two of the witnesses portrayed the creature as dwarf-sized with a large, oddly shaped head, skinny arms with long fingers and large eyes. This countenance notably resembles that of countless

reports of extraterrestrial sightings and suggests the possibility of UFO-related phenomena. It should be noted, however, that there were no UFO sightings reported during the time of the encounters.

There have been numerous theories proposed to explain what the witnesses might have seen, including an escaped monkey, a newborn foal, a young moose or a sick animal (such as a fox) that lost its hair. Others have gone so far as to suggest that the teens may have orchestrated an elaborate hoax to liven up the town.

Interestingly, aside from the aforementioned similarity to typical space-alien lore, the case of the Dover Demon bears an uncanny resemblance to a Native American legend known as the Mannegishi or Maymaygwayshi—a race of little people with big heads and long skinny arms and legs said to live near the water and play tricks on travelers.

See also *Mannegishi*, page 169.

The Gloucester Sea Serpent

CHARACTERISTICS: Long, snakelike body with prominent humps, dark in color with a light underbelly; moves in an undulating manner

SIZE: Over one hundred feet long; at least two feet in diameter at the thickest point

HABITAT: Atlantic Ocean off the northeastern tip of Massachusetts

APPETITE: Fish and other marine life

PRECAUTIONS: While most sea serpent reports do not suggest aggressive behavior, there have been a few instances where animals thought to be serpents have charged boats. As with any unknown marine life, caution is advised.

"You're gonna need a bigger boat."

—Police Chief Martin Brody in *Jaws*

Sightings of sea serpents in the Atlantic Ocean have occurred since settlers first came to inhabit the Massachusetts Bay Colony. In the 1800s, sightings became more and more frequent. In August of 1817, sea serpents were observed by approximately one hundred witnesses in one week.

This activity led a group named the Linnean Society of New England to begin a series of investigations with

hopes of proving the existence of a new species (*Scoliophis atlanticus*, the Atlantic humped snake). They tried a variety of tactics, from combing the beaches for evidence of sea serpent eggs to fashioning nets and traps with hopes of capturing a specimen. Finally the group examined a "baby serpent" found by a group of boys and claimed to have their evidence. The animal resembled a black snake with prominent humps. When the creature was later determined to actually *be* a black snake with prominent *tumors*, the group became the target of ridicule.

Sightings of the Gloucester Sea Serpent continued into the twentieth century, and sightings in other areas reinforce the possibility of sea serpents in the Atlantic. Resemblance to the Chesapeake Bay Monster suggests that this beast may be part of a larger species of marine animals.

See also *Chessie*, page 29.

Goatman

> **CHARACTERISTICS:** Legs of a goat, torso of a man, and horns; bears an uncanny resemblance to common depictions of Satan; also reported to carry an axe
>
> **SIZE:** Five to six feet tall
>
> **HABITAT:** Lovers' lanes and secluded highways in Maryland
>
> **APPETITE:** Omnivorous
>
> **PRECAUTIONS:** By all accounts, Goatman is dangerous—often homicidal.

The Goatman legend surrounding Prince George's County, Maryland, sounds like the stuff of urban legend. The crux of the story is that a scientist experimenting with goats somehow became mutated into a human–goat hybrid and was driven into seclusion because of his gruesome visage. Angered to the point of insanity by his alienation, Goatman began to exact vengeance on the youth of Maryland by attacking young lovers in their cars using an axe.

This wild tale has many variations, but reports of a creature fitting Goatman's description have persisted since the 1950s. It is said that the braying of Goatman can be heard from a bridge known as "Crybaby Bridge" on Governor Bridge Road near Bowie, Maryland (though another legend credits the shrill cries to an infant ghost who was drowned by her young mother beneath the bridge).

Legends aside, Maryland's Goatman sightings may be part of a larger phenomena, as encounters with

"goatmen" have also been reported in Alabama, Texas, Kentucky, Oregon, Oklahoma and California.

See also *The Lake Worth Monster,* page 132.

The Jersey Devil

> **CHARACTERISTICS:** Bat-like wings, lithe body, thin neck, goatlike horns, cloven hooves and slender tail
>
> ---
>
> **SIZE:** Reports range from three to six feet tall, 70 to 180 pounds
>
> ---
>
> **HABITAT:** Pine Barrens of New Jersey
>
> ---
>
> **APPETITE:** Carnivorous—preys upon small animals, livestock and occasionally human children
>
> ---
>
> **PRECAUTIONS:** Bright lanterns have been reported to deter Jersey Devil attacks. A crucifix, Bible or other holy items may also ward off the creature.

Originally known as the Leeds Devil, the Jersey Devil inhabits the desolate area of New Jersey known as the Pine Barrens. The monster is a ferocious predator with a demonic appearance. It is reported to resemble a mixture of several different animals, having the horns of a goat, the face and neck of a mule, leathery bat wings and cloven hooves. The Jersey Devil's diet most likely consists primarily of small animals such as rabbits and opossums, but it frequently wanders into more populated areas where it kills and mutilates livestock such as sheep or

cattle. Legend has it that the monster is fond of invading people's homes by swooping down the chimney and terrorizing families, often dragging screaming children from their beds and carrying them away into the night. The monster is also reported to have attacked cars, ripping the roofs off and abducting the passengers.

There are several different legends surrounding the origin of the Jersey Devil, but they all seem to have common elements. The basic premise of the legend is that in the mid-1700s the monster was born when a woman of the surname Leeds (or possibly a woman who lived in Leeds Point, New Jersey) gave birth to a cursed child. The details vary—some saying the child was cursed by the townspeople and others saying that the mother cursed the child herself. In either case, the monster leapt forth from her womb, devoured her other children and then flew up the chimney.

The beast has terrorized the New Jersey Pine Barrens ever since and has been seen by over two thousand witnesses, including naval hero Stephen Decatur (who shot at the monster with a cannonball when it flew over an ironworks factory) and Joseph Bonaparte (former King of Spain and brother of Napoleon who sighted the Jersey Devil on his New Jersey estate where he had settled under the name of Comte de Survilliers). Some believe that seeing the Jersey Devil is a portent of impending disaster. It has been seen before shipwrecks and wars.

There are striking similarities between descriptions of the Jersey Devil and Devil Monkey, Phantom Kangaroo and El Chupacabra sightings, which suggests that these monsters may actually be the same or part of a related cryptid species.

See also *Devil Monkeys,* page 190; *Phantom Kangaroos,* page 195; and *El Chupacabra,* page 183.

Manitou

CHARACTERISTICS: Dwarfish fairies with small horns or antlers

SIZE: Unspecified

HABITAT: Northeastern United States and Canada

APPETITE: Most likely nuts, berries and small woodland game

The Manitou are woodland faeries with small horns or antlers known to the Algonquin Indians. They are not necessarily malicious toward humans, though they do have a reputation as tricksters. Like Native Americans, the Manitou live in tribes. They are capable of using magic that they create through drumming and music.

Another Algonquin legend tells of a trickster named Wee-sa-kee-jac, or "Whiskey-Jack," that is sometimes associated with the Manitou. Whiskey-Jack has the head of a coyote and is well known for causing mischief.

Memphre

CHARACTERISTICS: Dark serpentine body with a long neck; appears as humps or coils in the water

-----

SIZE: Twenty to seventy feet long

HABITAT: Lake Memphremagog, bordering Vermont and Quebec

APPETITE: Fish

Memphre, a lake serpent named for its home in Lake Memphremagog, is by most accounts an archetypal lake serpent. The first modern sighting of Memphre was reported in 1816, and since then residents and tourists alike have seen the monster regularly. By most accounts, Memphre is a fairly docile creature and is usually seen lolling about in the water, though the Native Americans warned early settlers not to swim in the lake because of the beast's presence.

Memphre has inspired quite a bit of research. A historian and diver named Jacques Boisvert dedicated a good deal of his life to searching for the serpent. Founder of the International Society of Dracontology of Lake Memphremagog, a group dedicated to the search for lake monsters, he collected historical accounts and eyewitness testimonies and conducted daily diving expeditions in hopes of encountering Memphre. Boisvert passed away in 2006 at the age of 73, leaving behind a legacy for monster hunters everywhere and a colorful slice of Vermont history.

Nagumwasuck

CHARACTERISTICS: Incredibly ugly with little hair, beady eyes and pointed nose

---

SIZE: Approximately seven inches tall

HABITAT: Coastal Maine (and Nova Scotia)

APPETITE: Fish and small game, supplemented with acorns and berries

----

PRECAUTIONS: These creatures are shy and have become mistrusting of humans throughout the years, as we have driven them to the brink of extinction.

The Nagumwasuck are woodland faeries that befriended the Passamaquoddy Indians. While extremely ugly, these creatures are peaceful and usually hide from humans. They have on occasion been known to help travelers who are hunting or fishing and are thought of by the Passamaquoddy as good luck. The Nagumwasuck are very self-conscious about their appearance and should not be laughed at.

The New Jersey Lizard Man

CHARACTERISTICS: Tall humanoid biped with thick, green, lizard-like skin, reptilian features and red eyes

SIZE: Approximately seven feet tall

HABITAT: Newton/Lafayette area of New Jersey

APPETITE: Unknown

PRECAUTIONS: While there are no reports of attacks by the New Jersey Lizard Man, lizard men across the country have been known to exhibit aggressive behavior and seem to be fond of chasing after automobiles.

During the summer of 1973, reports of an alligator-like humanoid creature circulated in New Jersey. The creature bore similarities to a regional Native American legend that told of a giant man-sized fish that couldn't be caught.

Reptilian men of varying descriptions have been spotted in many areas of North America including Ontario, New York, Kentucky, South Carolina, Georgia, Florida and Ohio. Whether or not these sightings are part of a larger phenomenon is unknown.

See also *South Carolina Lizard Man,* page 78; *Loveland Frogman,* page 98; and *Gatormen,* page 56.

Oggie

CHARACTERISTICS: Amphibious, resembling a giant salamander

SIZE: Anywhere from five to twenty feet in length

HABITAT: Onondaga Lake near Syracuse, New York

APPETITE: Unknown

PRECAUTIONS: If searching for this monster, it is important to know that Onondaga Lake is considered to be one of the most polluted lakes in the United States. There is probably greater danger to you from the lake itself than from its monster.

During the late 1970s, people began noticing curious motions on the surface of Onondaga Lake, and a local Cub Scout troop reported seeing a dragon-like creature in the water. Area Native American legends spoke of a

lake serpent that would occasionally travel on land and terrorize families. They built fortifications to protect themselves from these creatures.

A more entertaining explanation, however, arose from the more recent history surrounding the lake. During the late nineteenth century as Syracuse became industrialized, Lake Onondaga became highly polluted. An unwanted pet salamander is thought to have been flushed and made its way through the sewers and into the lake, where the toxic chemicals in the water mutated the poor creature into a giant writhing monstrosity.

Old Greeny

CHARACTERISTICS: Green in color, this lake serpent has often been compared to an eel.

SIZE: Fifteen to thirty feet long

HABITAT: The Finger Lakes near Ithaca, New York

APPETITE: Probably fish

PRECAUTIONS: This monster is reported to have powerful jaws and has been blamed for attacking a swimmer and breaking his arm.

Plenty of legends and folklore surround Cayuga Lake and nearby Seneca Lake, including unexplained drums or cannon-like sounds that have been heard throughout history that the Indians attributed to a thunder god.

Like any self-respecting lake, Cayuga has its own serpentine monster. Old Greeny, as the monster is called, has an eel-like appearance and is suspected of having attacked swimmers. There are theories that the creature may be part of a group of lake serpents that have made their way through subterranean channels that connect the Cayuga and Seneca lakes. Interestingly, acoustics issuing from these channels have been suggested as an explanation for the aforementioned drumlike sounds surrounding the lakes. The existence of underground channels has never been confirmed.

Squonk

> **CHARACTERISTICS:** Incredibly ugly, with loose skin covered by warts and blemishes
>
> ---
>
> **SIZE:** Two to three feet tall
>
> ---
>
> **HABITAT:** Wooded areas of Pennsylvania
>
> ---
>
> **APPETITE:** Forest vegetation
>
> ---
>
> **PRECAUTIONS:** This creature is harmless, but encounters should be avoided, as you will cause it to weep itself to death.

Perhaps the saddest monster of all is the Squonk. This pitiful creature of Pennsylvania folklore causes no trouble whatsoever. The Squonk is merely ugly. Covered with floppy, fatty mole-covered skin, the Squonk is hyperaware of its own appearance and spends most of its time weeping and lamenting its misfortune. Whenever encountered by humans, the poor beast simply weeps until it dissolves into a puddle of tears.

The Winsted Wildman

CHARACTERISTICS: Tall humanoid covered with blond or brown hair

SIZE: About six feet tall, weighing around two hundred pounds

HABITAT: Wilderness areas surrounding Winsted, Connecticut

APPETITE: Unknown

PRECAUTIONS: Typically shy of contact with humans, any attempt to approach the creature is not advised. Contact should be made with extreme caution.

A hairy wildman bearing resemblance to Yeti lore of the Himalayas is said to roam Litchfield County in northern Connecticut. Sightings of the creature have been recorded since the late 1800s. It has a thin coat of hair of blond or light brown color (unlike the thick, dark matted coats possessed by Bigfoot and other Sasquatch-related animals). The Winsted Wildman typically avoids contact with people but is occasionally seen roaming woodland areas near bodies of water. The creature does have a tendency to lurk around "lover's lane" type areas and seems to have a fascination with teen mating rituals. If startled, the Wildman is known to flee making a series of yelps and whooping sounds.

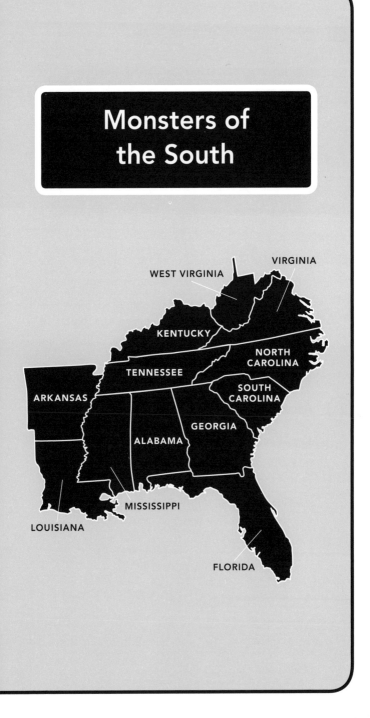

Monsters of the South

WEST VIRGINIA

VIRGINIA

KENTUCKY

NORTH CAROLINA

TENNESSEE

ARKANSAS

SOUTH CAROLINA

GEORGIA

ALABAMA

MISSISSIPPI

LOUISIANA

FLORIDA

Abominable Swamp Slob

CHARACTERISTICS: Hairy humanoid with three-toed feet

SIZE: Anywhere from five to ten feet tall

HABITAT: Swamps of the southeastern United States

APPETITE: Omnivorous

PRECAUTIONS: Typically thought to be aggressive

Abominable Swamp Slob, or A.S.S., is a regional name for a group of Bigfoot-like creatures more commonly referred to as Skunk Apes. The name is a derivative of the infamous Abominable Snowman of the Himalayas.

See also *Skunk Ape,* page 75; *Nape,* page 72; and *Abominable Snowman,* page 208.

Altamaha-Ha

The Altamaha-Ha is a large, dark-colored, two-humped serpentine monster said to inhabit the Altamaha River near the small fishing town of Darien, Georgia. First reported in the 1960s, the beast has been seen on numerous occasions by seasoned fishermen.

The Everglades Skunk Ape

> **CHARACTERISTICS:** Tall, foul-smelling apelike creature
>
> ---
>
> **SIZE:** Approximately seven feet tall, weighing three hundred pounds
>
> ---
>
> **HABITAT:** Florida's Everglades
>
> ---
>
> **APPETITE:** Omnivorous
>
> ---
>
> **PRECAUTIONS:** Like all swamp monsters, the Everglades Skunk Ape may be dangerous if confronted.

The Everglades Skunk Ape is most likely a member of the Skunk Ape family (see *Skunk Ape,* page 77). The monster fits the description of most tall, hairy, three-toed swamp monsters. Like the Skunk Ape, the Everglades Skunk Ape is surrounded by a fetid odor—some believe the creature lives in abandoned alligator caves in the swamps, and the smell is caused by waste from the gators. The Everglades Skunk Ape is believed to have a primarily vegetarian diet, though the beast has been blamed for deer killings in which only the liver has been eaten. Hunters in the Everglades claim that the creature also likes to steal pots full of lima beans.

The Flatwoods Monster

> **CHARACTERISTICS:** Dark green body; has a round red face surrounded by a pointed hoodlike object;

appears to wear a robe-like garment with folds around the bottom

---

SIZE: Approximately ten feet tall

HABITAT: Flatwoods, West Virginia

APPETITE: Unknown

PRECAUTIONS: Emits a noxious odor that may cause irritation of the skin and eyes, as well as nausea.

On September 12, 1952, a UFO was reported to have crashed on a small farm in Braxton County, West Virginia. That incident alone would draw the attention of any paranormal enthusiast, but the events that followed made the small town of Flatwoods the site of one of the most notorious UFO-related monster incidents in history.

The "crash" occurred in an area known as the Bailey Fisher Farm. A group of boys witnessed the spectacle while playing football and decided to investigate, only to be confronted by a towering green figure with a red face and glowing eyes. Its head appeared to be surrounded by some sort of pointed helmet or hood. The creature had clawed hands and gave off a chemical odor that was described as "sulfurous" or "metallic." Wisely, the boys fled. Other residents in the area also claimed to have caught glimpses of the unearthly figure. The area was later investigated to reveal some strange oily skid marks that were unable to be identified.

Most believe that the creature is a space alien that was somehow connected to the UFO crash. The beast has come to be known by several different names: the Flatwoods Monster, the Braxton County Monster, the Green Monster and the Phantom of Flatwoods.

Many suspect that the Flatwoods phenomenon is merely a bunch of wild rumors generated by a group of terrified boys who witnessed a meteor and then were frightened by a very scary owl. Others believe that an event comparable to the Roswell, New Mexico cover-up[1] occurred and has been swept under the rug

1 In the summer of 1947, a UFO reportedly crashed in Roswell, New Mexico. Debris from what some believed to be a flying saucer was reported to the authorities by a ranch hand. The military stepped in and summarily recovered the wreckage, which they stated was an experimental weather balloon. The incident has fueled a great deal of controversy and has been the subject of countless books, documentary films and television shows concerning UFOs.

by the government, the real events having been confused with intentional disinformation.

Whatever happened, the town of Flatwoods has made the most of it. There are billboards and memorabilia bearing the likeness of the eerie visitor, and in 2002, the town held a large festival celebrating the fiftieth anniversary of the appearance of the monster.

The West Virginia location, UFO-related circumstances and descriptions of the creature suggest that there may be a correlation between the Flatwoods Monster and the infamous Mothman (see *Mothman, page 68*).

The Fouke Monster

CHARACTERISTICS: Tall, three-toed, apelike biped covered with dark brown or black fur

---

SIZE: Six to ten feet tall; approximately three hundred pounds

---

HABITAT: The Sulphur River bottoms of Miller County, Arkansas

---

APPETITE: Carnivorous

PRECAUTIONS: While the Fouke Monster has never actually harmed anyone, it has been known to approach them and try to force its way into homes. It should be considered dangerous.

Said to inhabit the swampy areas surrounding Fouke, Arkansas, the Fouke Monster is probably one of America's most well-known monsters because of the 1970s cult film *The Legend of Boggy Creek*. The movie is a documentary-style film with dramatic recreations of the events surrounding the Fouke Monster legend, performed by many of the actual townspeople (most of them of the surname Crabtree) who have encountered the monster—all set to a serene folk music soundtrack. It is arguably one of the best worst movies of all time.

The Fouke Monster is described in typical swamp monster fashion—tall and massive with long matted hair, three-toed footprints and a putrid stench (often described as smelling like urine). The residents of Fouke report that the beast issues a bloodcurdling howl that sounds like a cross between that of an angry panther and a wounded cow. The creature is known to stalk livestock and feeds on chickens, hogs and even calves. Local hunters have used dogs to try to track the Fouke Monster to no avail, and reports of the monster's existence continue to this day.

While sometimes considered part of Bigfoot or Sasquatch lore, there are differences. For example, like humans, Bigfoot has five toes … the Fouke Monster only has three. The descriptions of the Fouke Monster have much in common with other swamp monster legends, lending some credence to theories that these monsters may be related, possibly a species.

See also *Honey Island Swamp Monster,* page 58; *Skunk Ape,* page 75; and *Nape,* page 72.

Gatormen

> **CHARACTERISTICS:** Upper body of a small human or a chimp, lower body of an alligator; greenish in color with scales covering the body
>
> ---
>
> **SIZE:** Four to six feet long
>
> ---
>
> **HABITAT:** Swamplands from eastern Texas to Florida
>
> ---
>
> **APPETITE:** Carnivorous—normally eat deer, turtles, frogs and whatever else they can find in the swamp

The existence of Gatormen has been reported since the 1700s. These creepy-looking creatures have the upper torso of a small human and the lower body of an alligator, complete with a tail and stubby gator legs. Despite their grotesque appearance, Gatormen are said to be very intelligent. They live and hunt together in small tribes and communicate with a primal language of guttural noises. They possess opposable thumbs and are known to fashion rudimentary tools and weapons.

Gatormen are probably most well known for a photograph of a gnarled-looking half-man/half-alligator carcass that occasionally makes an appearance on the

cover of the *Weekly World News*. The photo is actually of a mummified Gatorman named Jake who is the main attraction at Marsh's Free Museum in Long Beach, Washington.

Honey Island Swamp Monster

CHARACTERISTICS: Tall, humanoid biped with brown or gray matted hair, amber-colored eyes

SIZE: Over seven feet tall, weighing four hundred to five hundred pounds

HABITAT: The remote areas of the Honey Island Swamp, Louisiana

APPETITE: Carnivorous

PRECAUTIONS: As with all swamp monsters, this beast can be aggressive and should be considered a danger to livestock, pets and humans.

Covering approximately seventy thousand acres with nearly half of that being a government-sanctioned wildlife preserve, Louisiana's Honey Island Swamp is considered one of America's wildest and most unspoiled river swamps. The area is teeming with a plethora of animal life including bears, red wolves, cougars, wild boars and plenty of snakes and alligators. It is also the home of a creature known as the Honey Island Swamp Monster.

Sometimes referred to as "Wookie"[2] by locals, the Honey Island Swamp Monster fits the typical swamp monster bill. It is a tall, hairy creature that walks upright and inhabits the quiet, desolate areas of the swamp.

The creature was discovered in 1974 by a pair of hunters who discovered strange footprints next to the remnants of a slaughtered wild boar. The next day

2 *Wookie* is the name of a fictional race of tall, lumbering hairy creatures in the popular *Star Wars* films. Chewbacca, loyal sidekick to Han Solo and copilot of the spaceship known as the Millennium Falcon, is a wookie.

the pair met the beast itself, describing it as having dirty gray hair, wide-set yellow eyes and giving off a terrible smell of decay and death.

One of the hunters, Harlan E. Ford, went on to continue searching for evidence of the monster's existence until his death in 1980. He made plaster casts of the creature's footprints and made numerous attempts to capture the beast on camera. Ford's granddaughter Dana Holyfield, a journalist and photographer, has had a lifelong fascination with the monster and wrote a book that recounts the facts surrounding the legend.

Judging from Ford's plaster casts of the monster's footprints, the Honey Island Swamp Monster has three large toes and one smaller one. Other swamp monsters such as the Fouke Monster and the Skunk Ape are believed to have three toes. Aside from the differing number of toes, descriptions of all of these creatures are strikingly similar.

See also *Fouke Monster,* page 54; *Skunk Ape,* page 75; and *Nape,* page 72.

The Hopkinsville Goblins

CHARACTERISTICS: Glowing silver-colored body, large eyes on the sides of the head, pointed ears, wide mouths and clawlike fingers

----

SIZE: Approximately three feet tall

HABITAT: Areas surrounding Hopkinsville, Kentucky

The creatures known as the Hopkinsville Goblins, or Kelly-Hopkinsville Goblins, are a legend in UFO-related studies. Reports of them come solely from an encounter on August 21, 1955, when the Sutton/Lankford family of Kelly, Kentucky, found themselves under siege as the alien creatures attacked.

The incident began when Billy Ray Taylor (a friend who lived with the Suttons) witnessed a UFO land behind the farm. The family believed he was joking or had only seen a shooting star—but they would believe Billy Ray soon enough. An hour later, the family dog began barking and yelping in fear as a glowing figure appeared in the window. The men in the family grabbed their guns and fired at the creature, which seemed unharmed. Soon more creatures appeared and the family found themselves under attack. The Goblins were scratching at the windows, crawling on the roof and throwing rocks at the farmhouse. The family battled the creatures for about four hours before fleeing in their cars to nearby Hopkinsville, where they told their wild story to the local police.

Believing something had indeed terrified the poor family, the police chief rallied the local and state police. Newsmen, photographers and even military police swarmed the scene. No evidence of the Goblins was found, though no one could argue with all the bullet holes found fired by the terrified farmers. After investigating for several hours to no avail, the authorities withdrew about 3:00 A.M. No sooner than they left and the family settled in to try to sleep did the creatures reappear at the windows, forcing the terrified family to defend themselves all night long. The creatures disappeared at dawn and were never seen again.

It is said that the Sutton/Lankford family was forced to move as investigators and curious people flocked

to their farm after the attack, leaving them no peace whatsoever. Some believe, however, that the unfortunate family was abducted by either the government or by aliens.

Knobby

> **CHARACTERISTICS:** Tall, hairy, apelike creature with a small head and flat face
>
> ----
>
> **SIZE:** Approximately six feet tall, weighs two hundred pounds
>
> ----
>
> **HABITAT:** Cleveland County, North Carolina
>
> ----
>
> **APPETITE:** Omnivorous
>
> ----
>
> **PRECAUTIONS:** May be dangerous if cornered or startled; should be considered a threat to pets and livestock

Knobby, or Ol' Knobby, is the name given to a creature seen in wilderness areas in the vicinity of Toluca, North Carolina. The creature is most likely a member of a group of animals referred to by cryptozoologists as Napes (see *Nape,* page 72).

There were a large number of reported sightings of Knobby in the late 1970s that coincide with a number of instances where goats and other livestock were killed. Residents reported seeing the apelike beast and hearing its haunting howls, which were said to sound like a cross between the screams of a woman and the cries of a mountain lion.

Lake Murray Monster

First sighted in the 1930s, a prehistoric-looking snake-like monster reportedly inhabits Lake Murray near Irmo, South Carolina. The beast is fondly known as "Messie"—an obvious nod to the famous monster of Scotland's Loch Ness.

The Lake Norman Monster

> **CHARACTERISTICS:** Long and serpentine, with fins and flippers
>
> **SIZE:** Fifteen to thirty feet long
>
> **HABITAT:** Lake Norman, North Carolina
>
> **APPETITE:** Probably fish
>
> **PRECAUTIONS:** Is known to attack skiers and swimmers and emits a poisonous slime that may cause skin irritation.

Created in 1967 by the building of the Cowans Ford Hydroelectric Station on the Catawba River, Lake Norman is the largest body of freshwater in North Carolina. It boasts approximately five hundred miles of shoreline and is over one hundred feet deep in some

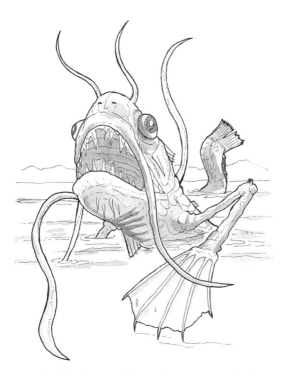

areas. The lake is owned by Duke Energy and is home to the McGuire Nuclear Plant. Though the lake is man-made, there have been reports of a strange creature lurking in the depths.

The Lake Norman Monster (also known as "Normie") is often described as long and serpentine with scaly fins or flippers. The creature has been seen by dozens of witnesses: swimmers, fishermen, campers, water-skiers and scuba divers. Descriptions vary in color and size, but it seems people are definitely seeing something large and frightening in the lake.

Normie isn't shy—the creature is fond of chasing fast boats and often bumps up against water-skiers and swimmers. There have even been attacks. A scuba

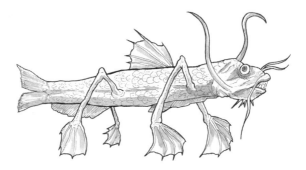

diver reported narrowly escaping a creature with a doglike head and red eyes that chomped onto one of his flippers. In another incident, a person on a jet ski claimed that a monster surfaced in front of him and brushed against his leg, leaving a slimy substance that caused an itchy rash.

There are several theories to explain the Lake Norman Monster phenomenon. Some believe the creature is a catfish of gigantic proportions (see *Giant Catfish,* page 193). Others think people are seeing large fish called bowfin, alligators or possibly large salamanders known as hellbenders, which can reach up to two feet in length. Of course, the typical "prehistoric" crocodilian theories abound as well, but my personal favorite is that Normie is a mutant fish created by pollution from the nuclear plant—after all, the lake is man-made, so shouldn't its monster be, too?

The Loup-Garou

> **CHARACTERISTICS:** Werewolf-like creature, often described as part fox or dog instead of wolf

HABITAT: Areas surrounding New Orleans

APPETITE: Cannibalistic

PRECAUTIONS: Like any werewolf, the Loup-Garou is said to hunt and devour humans.

A Cajun werewolf named after a French-Canadian legend of the same name, a Loup-Garou is a human cursed to change into a wolflike creature and prey upon men. According to some accounts, the person is forced to roam as a werewolf for a certain period of time—usually 101 nights—and may be released from the curse if someone he knows recognizes him as a Loup-Garou and draws his blood, but neither may speak of it until the time of the curse has passed.

See also *Werewolf,* page 205.

Mothman

CHARACTERISTICS: Dark humanoid with large wings and glowing red eyes

---

SIZE: Approximately six feet tall

HABITAT: Areas surrounding Point Pleasant, West Virginia

APPETITE: Unknown

PRECAUTIONS: Encounters with Mothman may cause effects similar to radiation burns. Inflammation of the eyes is often experienced. Seeing Mothman is a portent of impending disaster.

Beginning in November of 1966, the town of Point Pleasant, West Virginia, became the focus of a series of bizarre events that would terrorize the town for a year. Everything began with the sighting of a large flying creature with reflective red eyes by two young couples who were driving near an abandoned munitions factory from World War II. Surprised and frightened, the group sped away, but the monster followed their car until they reached the city limits. All members of the party described the figure as tall and dark in color (gray or brown) with large wings that unfolded from its back. They claimed they were driving a full one hundred miles per hour in an attempt to escape the beast and it had no trouble flying after them. The local authorities treated the matter seriously,

stating that all the witnesses were credible and genuinely frightened.

Local newspapers began covering the story and referred to the creature as "The Bird." People flocked to the old munitions factory, known by locals as the TNT Area, hoping to catch a glimpse of the mysterious winged man. The Bird didn't disappoint. It made numerous appearances: rising up from behind parked cars, chasing automobiles, creeping around nearby homes and peering into windows. In addition to sightings of the creature, a wave of UFO reports plagued areas surrounding Point Pleasant. People were seeing a variety of weird lights and shapes in the sky. The town was gripped in fear and became the focus of national attention. The creature became known as Mothman.

The strange happenings attracted the attention of paranormal researcher John Keel, who began documenting the whole affair with the help of local news reporter Mary Hyre (who covered countless Mothman sightings). The resulting book, *The Mothman Prophecies*, is an in-depth account that makes connections between the mysterious Mothman, the appearance of UFOs and the presence of strange men in black clothing who began interrogating and sometimes threatening witnesses. In 2002, the book was loosely adapted into a film starring Richard Gere, Laura Linney and Debra Messing.

Sightings of Mothman and the mysterious men in black continued until December 15, 1967, when the Silver Bridge connecting Point Pleasant and Gallipolis, Ohio, collapsed, plunging over thirty cars into the Ohio River and claiming the lives of forty-six people. Mothman wasn't seen after the incident, and many believe that its appearance was a portent of the impending tragedy.

The Mulberry Black Thing

CHARACTERISTICS: Descriptions vary wildly, but usually has red eyes and is always black in color

SIZE: Varies

HABITAT: Scenic areas in Kentucky along the Cumberland River

APPETITE: Unknown

In the backwoods of Kentucky, there is a very strange legendary entity known as the Mulberry Black Thing. It's hard to define the being as any sort of animal, as it seems to appear in different forms to anyone who sees it. It can appear as a bear- or panther-like animal, a large snake or even a strange oil slick. Witnesses typically sense the presence of the Mulberry Black Thing before they actually see it—the air becomes hazy and dense, and there is a sense of dead calm accompanied by a peculiar smell.

According to legends dating back to the early 1900s, the Mulberry Black Thing has an almost karma-like effect on those it encounters. Someone with evil in his heart might be mauled by a black bearlike creature in the woods, while some unfortunate lost traveler might be set back on her path by following a mysterious black serpent.

Some believe that the Mulberry Black Thing is psychic energy that is capable of taking form to act out its mysterious initiatives. Whatever this mysterious black "thing" might be, it appears it is a reflection of each individual's good or bad intentions and should be considered a reminder that we reap what we sow.

Nape

CHARACTERISTICS: Primate, descriptions vary

SIZE: Reports range widely; reported as being anywhere from the size of a chimp to a large gorilla

HABITAT: Various parts of North America, depending on species

APPETITE: Omnivorous

PRECAUTIONS: Reports vary, but animals described as Napes have been known to attack animals and frighten people.

The term *Nape*, or *NApe,* was coined by the well-known cryptozoologist Loren Coleman. It means North American Ape. Coleman, one of the strongest voices in legitimate cryptozoological research, came up with the name to encompass the wealth of reports of large primates dwelling in the valleys surrounding the Mississippi River and its tributaries.

Bigfoot, Sasquatch, Skunk Apes and various tall hairy monsters are considered by some to be part of the same or related phenomena. Others refer to Napes and Sasquatch differently, believing Napes to inhabit the southeastern United States where they reside in swamps and the wilderness surrounding river bottoms. Reports of southeastern Napes tend to portray the creatures as being violent (Sasquatch are often thought of as shy and tend to avoid humans). Napes are often accused of frightening people with their eerie howls, snatching away house pets and scaring even the fiercest of hunting dogs. They are often described as giving off a fetid stench.

Napes are primarily nocturnal. They tend to walk as bipeds and are known to be good swimmers.

See also *Fouke Monster,* page 54; *Skunk Ape,* page 75; and *Honey Island Swamp Monster,* page 58.

Sidehill Wampus

CHARACTERISTICS: Panther-like feline; travels in only one direction due to its uphill legs being shorter than its downhill ones

SIZE: Varies

HABITAT: Appalachian Mountains of Tennessee and western North Carolina

APPETITE: Carnivorous

PRECAUTIONS: It is important to note that there are two variations of this animal: the left-handed Sidehill Wampus and the right-handed Sidehill Wampus. When confronting this beast it is crucial to know which variation you have encountered—failure to know your right from your left may prove fatal.

The South is teaming with legends of mysterious, often supernatural felines. One particularly unusual creature is the Sidehill Wampus. This large cat is very fast and aggressive, and inhabits the mountains and hills of Appalachia. Very much like a panther or puma, the cat has one distinguishing feature—its specialized legs. Mountain life has adapted the Sidehill Wampus to have legs that are shorter on one side than the other. As a result, the beast can only travel in one direction.

The Sidehill Wampus has a fearsome cry and victims often make the mistake of trying to flee the creature, which is impossible. The correct way to evade this beast is to wait for its attack and then dodge it. If you can get past the Wampus, you will be safe, as the animal will simply roll down the mountain if it tries to turn to give chase. However, you must be careful not to run too far, for you may meet the Wampus again face-to-face as it comes back around the mountain.

Skunk Ape

> **CHARACTERISTICS:** Apelike biped covered with orange or reddish hair
>
> ---
>
> **SIZE:** Five to ten feet tall, weighing anywhere from three hundred to one thousand pounds
>
> ---
>
> **HABITAT:** Southeastern United States, particularly the swamps and wilderness of Florida

APPETITE: Omnivorous

PRECAUTIONS: This monster has been known to kill housecats and in one instance even threw a kitten at a witness when startled. One can only assume it is prone to extreme violence.

Skunk Ape, or Florida Skunk Ape, is the name given to a creature widely seen throughout the Florida wilderness and sometimes in other southern states. Descriptions of the Skunk Ape vary, some describing a large Bigfoot-like creature and some reporting that the animal is shorter in stature, looking much like an orangutan. The Skunk Ape is often described as having glowing orange or green eyes and gives off a foul odor that is

so repugnant that dogs often refuse to track the beast's scent (hence the unflattering name).

While this beast seems to prefer eating everything from wild pigs, deer and fledgling wading birds to household pets, studies of feces found near skunk ape sightings have concluded that it also ingests vegetable matter on occasion.

Skunk Apes have been sighted for decades by scores of witnesses. In 1997, two Everglades tour guides on separate occasions pointed out an individual creature to their tour groups, who corroborated the stories in both instances. In 1998, a campground owner named David Shealy captured twenty-seven photographs of a Skunk Ape over an eight-month vigil. Shealy has since devoted much of his life to researching the animals as head of the Skunk Ape Research Headquarters in Ochopee, Florida. He has collected plaster casts of the beasts' footprints and even collected a sample of Skunk Ape hair, which was reportedly later stolen by men wearing black suits with dark sunglasses driving a black sedan (see *Men in Black*, page 216).

Skunk Apes continue to make appearances. As recently as 2003, there was a rash of sightings that coincided with reports of over one hundred missing pets in Campbell County, Tennessee. Many theories have been put forward to explain Skunk Ape sightings. Some believe the animals are relatives of the Sasquatch of the Pacific Northwest. Others believe Skunk Apes are simply primates that have either escaped from zoos or have somehow gone undetected in the wild. Others believe the creature is part of a group of swamp monsters known for their three-toed footprints and eerie howls.

See also *Fouke Monster,* page 54; *Honey Island Swamp Monster,* page 58; and *Nape,* page 72.

The South Carolina Lizard Man

CHARACTERISTICS: Tall biped with three clawed fingers and toes, reptilian skin and red eyes

SIZE: Approximately seven feet tall

HABITAT: Areas surrounding the swamps of South Carolina

APPETITE: Carnivorous

PRECAUTIONS: This creature is massive, can move incredibly fast and is prone to unprovoked violence.

During the summer of 1988, the small town of Bishopville, South Carolina, found itself in the middle of monster mania when a frightening reptilian beast revealed itself to hundreds of witnesses.

The South Carolina Lizard Man, also known as the Lizard Man of Scape Ore Swamp and the Lizard Man of Lee County, first made its presence known when it attacked a teenage boy who was changing a flat tire in the middle of the night after working a late shift at a fast-food establishment in Bishopville. Seventeen-

year-old Christopher Davis glanced up from the tire to see a large green monster with red eyes running full speed toward him. He jumped into the car and the beast threw itself onto the roof and began trying to claw its way inside. Davis sped away and eventually shook the creature off. The adventure left his car with plenty of claw marks and scratches. The driver's side mirror was wrenched off by the beast.

In the following months, the local sheriff received nonstop reports of Lizard Man sightings. They even had to set up a special hotline devoted to calls about the creature. By August of the same year, reports began to cease, though there are still reports from time to time. As recently as October of 2005, a woman reported seeing two Lizard Men in her yard. The officer on duty assured her that everything was okay and that the monsters "just like to check on humans from time to time." He probably never had one trying to claw its way through the roof of his car.

Wampus Cat

CHARACTERISTICS: Resembles a mountain lion, but walks on its hind legs

SIZE: Approximately six feet tall

HABITAT: Eastern Tennessee and the Appalachian Mountains

APPETITE: Carnivorous

PRECAUTIONS: Like other large cats, the Wampus Cat is predatory and should be considered dangerous.

In the mountains of Appalachia, folks fear large cats. Phantom panthers are said to roam areas that mountain lions do not normally inhabit. These mysterious cats are legendary, and one such story is that of the Wampus Cat.

According to the legend, a beautiful Cherokee woman made the mistake of following her husband on a hunting trip. Thinking herself clever, she disguised herself in a cloak made of the fur of a mountain lion and set forth to spy upon the men of the tribe as they sat around the campfire telling stories of sacred magic—magic that was forbidden to women of the tribe. She was soon discovered and as punishment was cursed to wear her panther cloak and roam the hills forever. The screams of the Wampus Cat can be heard in the night as she cries in vain for the return of her human form.

Whitey

> **CHARACTERISTICS:** Serpentine with mottled skin and a spiny backbone
>
> ---
> **SIZE:** Approximately thirty feet long
>
> ---
> **HABITAT:** Arkansas' White River, particularly areas near Newport where the river is deepest
>
> ---
> **APPETITE:** Unknown

The White River Monster, affectionately known as Whitey, is widely accepted as real by townspeople of Newport, Arkansas. The creature has been encountered by fishermen and campers since 1915. Whitey is described as being snakelike and prehistoric in appearance. The monster is said to make a loud bellowing noise, but aside from this startling sound, it exhibits no aggressive behavior. Whitey seems content to spend its days floating along the river. In 1973, the Arkansas State Legislature created a refuge for the monster along the Jacksonport State Park area of the river, making it unlawful to harm or molest the creature.

Monsters of the Midwest

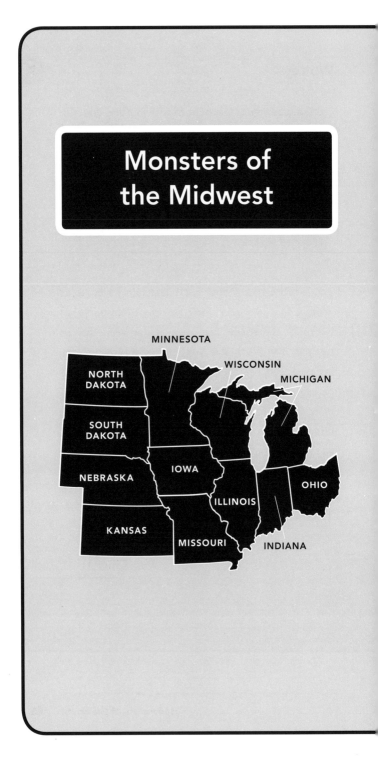

MINNESOTA

WISCONSIN

MICHIGAN

NORTH
DAKOTA

SOUTH
DAKOTA

NEBRASKA

IOWA

OHIO

ILLINOIS

KANSAS

MISSOURI

INDIANA

The Alkali Lake Monster

CHARACTERISTICS: Gray or brown in color, resembles an enormous alligator with a single horn protruding from its forehead

SIZE: Probably measures around forty to sixty feet in length, though some tales say the monster is three hundred feet long

HABITAT: Alkali Lake (also known as Walgren Lake), Nebraska

APPETITE: Carnivore

PRECAUTIONS: The monster is capable of devouring humans and emits an overpowering odor.

First officially reported in the early 1920s, the Alkali Lake Monster is also mentioned in Native American folklore and is sometimes referred to as Giganticus Brutervious—a name assigned to the monster by the Federal Writers' Project in Nebraska in a 1938 pamphlet concerning local folklore.

The Alkali Lake Monster is rumored to live in the lake but comes ashore to prey upon cattle and other livestock. It is alligator-like in appearance, save for the horn growing between its eyes. The reptilian beast emits a terrible odor, which according to Native American legend can prove fatal. Reports of the monster's size vary wildly. One skeptic ventured onto the lake to spend a night searching for the beast. When he returned, his hair had turned completely white and he was unable to speak for several days. When he finally regained his voice, he told of a beast three hundred feet in length and weighing over one hundred tons. More conservative accounts describe the creature as being about forty feet long.

Axehandle Hound

CHARACTERISTICS: Strange doglike creature with an axe-blade-shaped head and a thin, lanky body

---

SIZE: Two to four feet long

HABITAT: Midwest

APPETITE: Axe handles

PRECAUTIONS: You should never leave an axe unattended. It may become a snack for one of these odd hounds. (Plus, it's simply a dangerous thing to do!)

These folklore animals are rumored to have plagued pioneers and lumberjacks by eating the handles of their axes. The creatures have ravenous appetites and can consume dozens of axe handles in short periods of time. Aside from their annoying appetite, the beasts are shy of humans and are not particularly harmful.

The Beast of Bray Road

CHARACTERISTICS: Wolflike appearance; long forearms ending in clawed hands, grayish brown fur, yellow gleaming eyes; travels on its hind legs as well as on all fours

SIZE: Four to six feet tall

HABITAT: Southeastern Wisconsin

APPETITE: Carnivorous

PRECAUTIONS: Seems to have a habit of giving chase to moving vehicles and occasionally attacking motorists. Use caution when traveling in the area at night, particularly during a full moon.

During the 1980s and 1990s, Wisconsin became the home to numerous reports of creatures believed to be werewolves. Several of the sightings occurred in the areas surrounding the towns of Elkhorn and Delavan, particularly on Bray Road. Witnesses were usually motorists who reported seeing a creature resembling

a large wolf or hyena that seemed oddly hunched and in most cases was standing on two legs. The beast was rumored to have hands that looked almost human but ended in gruesome claws.

The first report of the creature involves a woman who stopped her car after running over something in the road. As she got out to investigate, a dark shape ran toward her and she quickly returned to her vehicle. As she sped away, the creature jumped onto the back of her car, clawing her trunk lid before finally falling off.

The case drew the interest of a Delavan-based newspaper reporter and artist Linda Godfrey, who broke the story and drew sketches of the monster. She went on to follow every sighting of the creature and wrote an in-depth book detailing the events titled *The Beast of Bray Road*.

While there is some possible connection between sightings of this creature to area Bigfoot-related reports, many believe the Beast of Bray Road to be an actual werewolf (see *Werewolves,* page 205). There are similarities between typical werewolf lore and Native American legends of skin-walkers—shamans capable of shape-shifting into animals such as wolves or coyote (see *Skin-walkers,* page 198). Others have speculated that the creature is a Shunka Warakin, a wolflike creature of Native American mythology (see *Shunka Warakin,* page 118).

In 2005 the tale of Bray Road's werewolf scare was made into an indie film directed by Leigh Scott, also titled *The Beast of Bray Road.* The film depicts a Wisconsin town full of people who find their favorite pastime of drinking alcoholic beverages interrupted when members of the one-bar drinking scene begin to turn up dismembered. [I do not recommend watching the film with your spouse or significant other unless you want to be reminded of it every time you try to pick a video for the next three months.]

The Beast of Busco

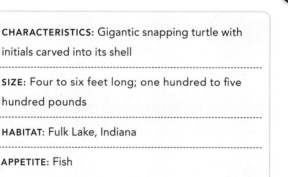

CHARACTERISTICS: Gigantic snapping turtle with initials carved into its shell

---

SIZE: Four to six feet long; one hundred to five hundred pounds

---

HABITAT: Fulk Lake, Indiana

APPETITE: Fish

Churubusco, Indiana, calls itself Turtle City. The town holds a festival known as Turtle Days each June with a carnival, parade and turtle races. All the hubbub is in honor of the giant turtle known as the Beast of Busco that reportedly lives in a small lake on one of the town's farms.

The legend began in 1898 when local farmer Oscar Fulk claimed that an oversized turtle was living in his lake. No one believed him until he sold the property and other people began to see the creature, which they nicknamed "Oscar" after the old man (some witnesses even claimed that the turtle bore the farmer's initials, which were carved into its shell). The creature surprised two unlucky fishermen in 1948 when it surfaced and stole their fishing poles. The incident sparked a rash of sightings that in turn caused a large-scale turtle hunt in 1949. Hunters, trappers and even a scuba diver from Chicago searched for the beast. The townsfolk tried repeatedly to catch Oscar using

guns, nets, chains, homemade traps fashioned from chicken wire and even a female sea turtle to lure the beast to the surface. In a last-ditch effort, the lake was drained to a depth of only five feet. There was no sign of Oscar and locals theorized that the creature had migrated to another lake or nearby river through underground channels.

Bildad

> **CHARACTERISTICS:** Legs like a kangaroo, webbed feet, a hawk-like beak and a flat tail like a beaver
>
> ---
>
> **SIZE:** Roughly the size of a beaver
>
> ---
>
> **HABITAT:** Midwest
>
> ---
>
> **APPETITE:** Fish

The Bildad (or Billdad) is a sphinx-like creature combining the attributes of a kangaroo, a beaver and a hawk. It lives along rivers, streams and ponds and uses its strange physiology to catch fish. The Bildad is fond of hiding in tall reeds until fish surface and uses its powerful legs to launch over the fish, smacking it on the head with its beaver-like tail and then gobbling it up with its sharp, hooked beak.

Charles Mill Lake Monster

> **CHARACTERISTICS:** Reptilian, with no apparent arms; luminous green skin and glowing green eyes
>
> -----
>
> **SIZE:** Approximately seven feet tall
>
> -----
>
> **HABITAT:** Charles Mill Lake, Mansfield, Ohio
>
> -----
>
> **APPETITE:** Unknown

On two occasions, once in 1959 and once in 1963, a strange armless reptilian creature has reportedly risen out of Mansfield's Charles Mill Lake. The creature leaves behind large webbed footprints and has been compared to the famous monster from the movie *Creature From the Black Lagoon*.

Little seems to be known about the creature other than its appearance, though its description does call to mind another Ohio monster, the Loveland Frogman (see *Loveland Frogmen,* page 98). Charles Mill Lake is also the home of the Bigfoot-esque monster known as Orange Eyes (see page 108).

Cole Hollow Road Monster

> **CHARACTERISTICS:** Tall, apelike creature with white hair and three-toed feet
>
> -----
>
> **SIZE:** Seven to eight feet tall, weighing over two hundred pounds

On May 25, 1972, police in Pekin and Peoria, Illinois, received over two hundred reports of a white apelike creature that left three-toed tracks and gave off a strong odor. The creature was first spotted near Cole Hollow Road and became known as the Cole Hollow Road Monster, or "Cohomo" for short. Sightings of the monster lasted through July and eventually led to an organized search involving one hundred volunteers. Unfortunately, the search was called off when one of the volunteers shot himself in the leg.

See also *Murphysboro Mud Monster,* page 107.

Devil's Lake Monster

CHARACTERISTICS: May possess octopus-like tentacles

SIZE: Undetermined

HABITAT: Devil's Lake, Wisconsin

APPETITE: Unknown

Devil's Lake, Wisconsin, is the home of a couple of monster-related Native American legends. A Sioux legend tells of an expedition of braves who were attacked when they launched their canoe onto the lake. The surface of the lake erupted in a flurry of tentacles, and all of the men were dragged beneath the churning water. The rest of the tribe heard their screams and ran to the shore to witness their collective demise.

Another legend from the Nakota tribe tells of a creature called Hokuwa that became trapped in shallow water. The beast had a long neck and a small head—a description that coincides with the plesiosaur theory to which so many lake monster sightings are attributed. The tribe observed the monster for several days before it was finally able to free itself and return to the depths.

The Enfield Horror

CHARACTERISTICS: Short grey creature with three legs and small forearms; capable of hopping long distances

SIZE: Four to five feet tall

HABITAT: Enfield, Illinois

APPETITE: Unknown

PRECAUTIONS: It has been known to try to force its way into homes—this creature should be considered aggressive.

First sighted in April of 1973, the Enfield Horror is a monkey-like creature with three legs that is fond of trying to claw its way into people's homes. The beast was seen and fired upon by several locals and amateur monster hunters during the month of May. Witnesses claimed that the creature was very fast and hopped like a kangaroo, covering as much as twenty-five feet in a single hop.

Descriptions of the Enfield Horror match those of creatures called Devil Monkeys by cryptozoologists.

See also *Devil Monkeys,* page 190; and *Phantom Kangaroos,* page 195.

The Farmer City Monster

CHARACTERISTICS: Tall, dark, hairy creature with gleaming yellow eyes

----

SIZE: Seven to eight feet tall, weighing over two hundred pounds

----

HABITAT: Farmer City, Illinois

APPETITE: Has been suspected of eating sheep

During July of 1970, there were numerous reports of a Bigfoot-like monster in areas surrounding Farmer City, Illinois. The beast was seen by dozens of people including a group of camping teenagers, construction workers and even a local police officer who encountered the creature when investigating a monster sighting. During the course of the month, the monster skulked around the woods, left human-looking tracks near the river and appeared in the headlights of cars only to flee into the nearby forest. All of the reports agreed—the creature walked on two legs and had bright yellow eyes.

Guyascutus

CHARACTERISTICS: Possesses legs of adaptable length

SIZE: Ten feet long

HABITAT: Midwestern hills and slopes

APPETITE: Unknown

The folklore monster known as Guyascutus has a few contradictory descriptions. The creature seems to be a sort of dragon of the Midwest, at times being described as a cross between an alligator and an armadillo, with fearsome teeth and dorsal spines. Other accounts tell of a sphinx-like creature combining the attributes of a deer and a rabbit. Whatever the case, one detail about the Guyascutus remains the same in all accounts: The beast has telescoping legs that can adjust in length to allow the animal to easily navigate sloping hills and mountainsides.

Hodag

CHARACTERISTICS: Black fur, horns like a bull, spikes along its back, and a spear-like tail

----

SIZE: Six feet long, three feet tall at the shoulder

HABITAT: Forests of Wisconsin

APPETITE: Unknown

PRECAUTIONS: Gores victims with its horns and spines.

Lumberjacks in nineteenth-century Wisconsin told of a frightening creature known as the Hodag. The creature had a large head with fearsome horns and a row of spikes protruding from its back. Reportedly there are a few different species of Hodag: the black Hodag (the most common, as well as the most vicious variety), the Sidehill Dodge Hodag (which has adapted to living on hillsides with a shorter set of legs on one side of its body), the Cave Hodag (which has glowing eyes and is able to see in the darkness of caves) and the Shovel-Nose Hodag (named for the spade-like bony growth on its nose).

Lake Leelanau Monster

> **CHARACTERISTICS:** Long neck that bears an uncanny resemblance to the branch of a dead tree
>
> -----
>
> **SIZE:** Ten to twenty feet in length
>
> -----
>
> **HABITAT:** Lake Leelanau, Michigan
>
> -----
>
> **APPETITE:** Unknown
>
> -----
>
> **PRECAUTIONS:** This creature may be difficult to spot, as it apparently has the ability to camouflage itself.

A curious lake monster sighting occurred in Leelanau County, Michigan, in 1910 that strangely bears little resemblance to a plesiosaur or zueglodon, the prehistoric usual suspects in most lake monster theories.

The sighting was made by a young man named William Gauthier. He was fishing in an outlet of Lake Leelanau that had been cut off by a dam built in the late 1800s in order to provide hydroelectric power to the Leland Sawmill. Gauthier rowed to an area of the lake where several dead cedar trees stuck out of the water and attempted to tie his boat to one of the branches. Suddenly the "branch" opened its eyes, dove beneath the water and swam away. According to Gauthier, other locals confessed to him that they too had seen the monster, though none would come forward publicly.

The most interesting detail of this particular monster sighting is the creature's ability to disguise itself—a characteristic that many animals possess, such as chameleon lizards or phasmids (insects that have adapted to resemble sticks or leaves in order to evade predators). For a firsthand account of a visit to Lake Leelanau, see page 238.

 ## The Loveland Frogmen

CHARACTERISTICS: Humanoids with thick leathery skin, frog-like features and wide, bulging eyes, webbed hands and feet

---

SIZE: Reports range from three to four feet tall; approximately fifty or sixty pounds

---

HABITAT: Areas surrounding the Ohio River—most sightings have occurred near Loveland, Ohio

APPETITE: Unknown

- -

PRECAUTIONS: While the frogmen are typically wary of humans, there are reports of swimmers being attacked from beneath the water that may be attributed to these creatures.

The Loveland Frogmen are often described as frog-like trolls. They typically inhabit the banks of the Ohio River, the nearby Little Miami River and surrounding areas. They seem to be fond of lying along the side of roads running along the riverbanks and have on occasion been mistaken for roadkill. Upon discovery, the creatures stand on two legs and flee to dive down the riverbank and back to the water.

These strange creatures were originally spotted in 1955 by a local businessman who claimed to have seen three of them underneath a bridge in Loveland, Ohio.

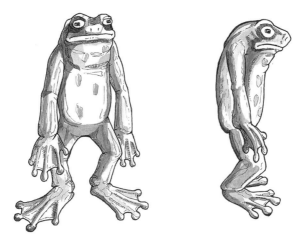

He claimed to have watched the Loveland Frogmen for a full three minutes before becoming frightened and leaving. In 1972, a police officer encountered one of the Loveland Frogmen while driving and nearly hit the creature as it darted in front of his vehicle, only to dive over a guardrail, leaving peculiar scrape marks on the riverbank. Two weeks later another police officer had a similar encounter—only he fired his revolver at the creature and apparently missed.

The Loveland Frogmen have been seen on occasion by area farmers, motorists and residents ever since. They seem to be most active during the spring of the year, and sightings are most likely to occur during the month of March.

The Manitou Monster

> **CHARACTERISTICS:** Serpentine
>
> ---
>
> **SIZE:** Sixty feet long
>
> ---
>
> **HABITAT:** Lake Manitou in Rochester, Indiana
>
> ---
>
> **APPETITE:** Unknown

Early settlers in the pioneer town of Logansport, Indiana, near present-day Rochester, had told tales of fearsome creatures living in area lakes. Local Indians believed that monsters lived in Lake Manitou because on occasion they would find gigantic bones along the lakeshore (geologists believe the bones were probably the fossilized bones of mastodons, which have been found in the area). In 1837, pioneer artist and reporter George Winter went to investigate the rumors for an article for the *Logansport Telegraph*. His article described a creature sixty feet in length, three feet in diameter, with large round eyes and a forked tongue. The Manitou Monster, as it came to be known, is still believed to lurk in the lake to this day.

The Minnesota Iceman

> **CHARACTERISTICS:** Hairy humanoid corpse frozen in a block of ice in a refrigerated glass coffin
>
> ---
>
> **SIZE:** Approximately six feet tall (ice block is 6' 11" long, 2' 8" wide and 3' 6" deep)

The Minnesota Iceman is the subject of much debate among cryptozoologists. The phenomenon revolves around a traveling sideshow exhibition that was circulating in the 1960s. The exhibit featured a frozen figure that was reportedly a prehistoric Iceman. In 1967, a college zoology major named Terry Cullen viewed the exhibit and thought the creature deserved closer examination. He contacted cryptozoologist Ivan T. Sanderson, who along with Bernard Heuvelmans (who has been called the "Father of Cryptozoology") conducted a three-day study of the specimen with the permission of exhibitor Frank Hansen.

The examination revealed some startling details. The pair declared that the specimen was indeed authentic, stating that a section of the ice had melted at some point and the exposed flesh gave off a rotting smell. They also concluded that the creature had died from a bullet wound to the right eye, meaning the creature was not a frozen man from the Ice Age at all

but instead a creature of undetermined species and of great interest to the field of cryptozoology.

Following the Sanderson and Heuvelmans study of the Iceman, the creature disappeared and was replaced with what Hansen later admitted was a fake. The exhibitor's story changed numerous times, growing more and more unbelievable. He claimed that he only ran the exhibit and the Iceman was actually owned by an anonymous Hollywood millionaire. He said that the millionaire had funded the creation of replicas to protect the real Iceman from damage or theft.

Many believe that the whole incident was a hoax and a real Minnesota Iceman never existed—but Sanderson and Heuvelmans took precise measurements and photographs and claimed there were at least fifteen specific technical differences between the original and the replica.

Theories of the origin of the Iceman vary. Some believe the creature is actually a Neanderthal that was killed in the Vietnam War and smuggled into the United States, somehow ending up in the possession of Hansen (who was an Air Force captain at the time). Other stories involve a Minnesota woman who claimed to have been raped by a Bigfoot-like creature while she was hunting in the woods. She finally escaped, killed the creature by shooting it in the eye with her rifle and fled, leaving the body in the woods (where it could have conceivably been discovered and frozen for sideshow display).

Replicas of the Iceman are still exhibited at sideshows and carnivals to this day. Some claim that the real Minnesota Iceman sometimes makes an appearance, though it is likely that it thawed, rotted and had to be disposed of.

Momo

CHARACTERISTICS: Tall biped with thick, matted black hair, three-toed feet

---

SIZE: Six to seven feet tall

HABITAT: Woodland areas surrounding Louisiana, Missouri

APPETITE: Dogs, livestock and the occasional peanut butter and jelly sandwich

---

PRECAUTIONS: Momo has a habit of trying to abduct small children and is known to kill pets and livestock.

The Missouri Monster, or Momo for short, has been spotted in Missouri's wooded areas along the Mississippi River since the 1940s. The creature is described as man-sized, with a carpet of long black hair. Its footprints show three toes on each foot. Momo gives off a putrid smell that has been compared to rotting flesh or stagnant river water. Exposure to the monster's stench has been known to cause extreme nausea—a dog was reported to have vomited for three hours after a Momo encounter.

Momo has been known to accost people, most likely looking for something to eat. The beast has

attacked picnickers and stolen their food, tried to kidnap children and is blamed for the death of pets and livestock—Momo seems to have a particular taste for dogs, going so far as to dig up graves of deceased pets to eat their remains.

The largest number of Momo sightings occurred in Louisiana, Missouri, during the summer and fall of 1972. The scare began on July 11 when the monster approached three children as they played in their backyard that bordered a wilderness area known as Marzolf Hills. The beast was covered with blood and was carrying a dead dog. Luckily, Momo was frightened away by the children's screams. The children's father, Edgar Harrison, with the help of the police chief and a posse of local men, began to search the area. The group eventually discovered several unearthed dog graves and a primitive shelter that was filled with the creature's noxious odor. Neighbors began reporting missing pets, hearing eerie howls and catching traces of Momo's scent.

Given descriptions of the monster's appearance and smell, Momo is most likely a member of or related to the species of monster known as the Skunk Ape or Nape.

See also *Skunk Ape,* page 77; and *Nape,* page 72.

Murphysboro Mud Monster

CHARACTERISTICS: Tall, apelike creature with white hair, usually covered in mud

SIZE: Seven to eight feet tall, weighing over two hundred pounds

HABITAT: Murphysboro, Illinois

APPETITE: Omnivorous

PRECAUTIONS: May be dangerous if cornered or startled

In late June of 1973, a light-colored Bigfoot-like creature terrorized the town of Murphysboro, Illinois. Also known as Big Muddy (named after the Big Muddy River on the outskirts of town), the Murphysboro Mud Monster surprised a couple in a parked car near a boat dock on the evening of June 25. According to the couple, the beast emerged from the woods screaming and covered with mud. Police searched the area and found a trail of thick, foul-smelling muddy slime.

The creature was seen the next evening by a couple of teenagers and also by workers at a nearby fairground who said they witnessed the beast as it stared at a pen full of tethered ponies.

The June 1973 sightings are not the only occurrences of Bigfoot-related activity in Illinois. In the previous three years, central Illinois police received countless reports of tall ape-like creatures skulking about.

See also *The Farmer City Monster,* page 93; and *The Cole Hollow Road Monster,* page 90.

Orange Eyes

> **CHARACTERISTICS:** Tall, hairy, apelike creature with glowing orange eyes
>
> ---
>
> **SIZE:** Eleven feet tall, weighing one thousand pounds
>
> ---
>
> **HABITAT:** Wooded areas in Mansfield, Ohio
>
> ---
>
> **APPETITE:** Unknown
>
> ---
>
> **PRECAUTIONS:** Any time you are parked in the vicinity of Ruggles Road, make sure you have protection.

First spotted in 1959, a large Bigfoot-like creature known as Orange Eyes is rumored to wander a secluded country road near Mansfield, Ohio's Charles Mill Reservoir. Ruggles Road is frequented as a "lover's lane" by area teenagers, and on several occasions amorous youths have been interrupted by eerie howls and the glow of the creature's bright orange eyes peering into their car windows. On a couple of occasions, townspeople have formed posses to try to track Orange Eyes—in 1968, a group of teens armed with ball bats, ropes and flashlights charged into the woods after the beast. All attempts to confront Orange Eyes have been unsuccessful.

The Piasa Bird

CHARACTERISTICS: Winged creature with scales, antlers, fierce teeth and a long, coiled tail with a poisonous barb

---

SIZE: Approximately the size of a deer or calf

HABITAT: Cliffs along the Mississippi River

APPETITE: Human flesh

PRECAUTIONS: This creature's name translates from the language of the Illini tribe to mean "Giant Bird That Devours Man." Enough said.

The Piasa, or Piasa Bird, is a legendary Native American monster that seems to be part bird, part snake with antlers, talons and a beard. According to legend, the creature acquired a taste for human blood during a war between Illini tribes. The beast and its mate began swooping down on villages to carry off children to devour in their caves or to drop off the sides of cliffs.

The image of the Piasa was first seen by French explorer Father Jacques Marquette during his Mississippi River expedition in the 1670s. The beast's visage was painted on a rock bluff over a waterfall near what

is now Alton, Illinois. Originally serving as a warning to travelers, this impressive painting has been restored by local citizens and today is a treasured historical landmark.

Descriptions of the creature and its murderous behavior link the Piasa Bird to the legendary Thunderbird.

See also *Thunderbird,* page 136.

Monsters of the West

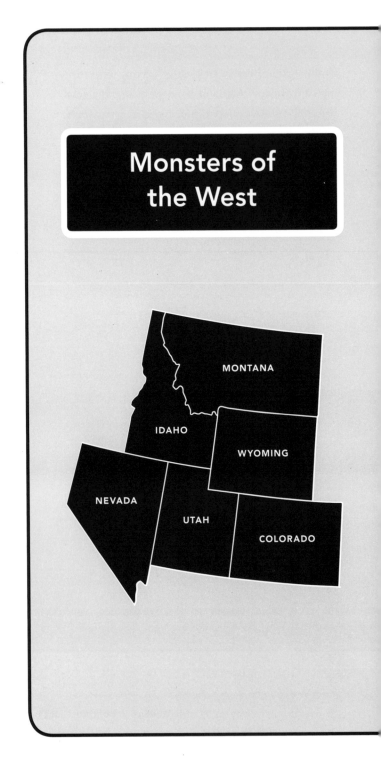

The Bear Lake Monster

> **CHARACTERISTICS:** Serpentine, brown in color with small ears protruding from the side of its head, flipper-like legs
>
> **SIZE:** Reports vary from forty to two hundred feet long
>
> **HABITAT:** Bear Lake in the northeast corner of Utah
>
> **APPETITE:** Carnivorous

The Bear Lake Monster is sometimes described in standard lake monster fashion as a serpent undulating in the water. Other reports tell of a creature that seems to be part serpent, part seal or walrus with a long, brown snaky body and short legs it uses to come up on shore.

First sighted in 1868 by Joseph Rich, son of a Mormon apostle who colonized the lake, the monster is a well-loved local legend. There is even a tall tale that recounts an epic battle between the Bear Lake Monster and folk hero Pecos Bill. According to the story, the fight lasted several days and caused a hurricane. In the end, Pecos Bill prevailed and flung the monster halfway around the world into Scotland's Loch Ness, where the creature became famous.

Apparently, the Pecos Bill story is only a myth because sightings of the Bear Lake Monster occur to this day. The monster seems to be a popular attraction for tourists. There is even a scenic folklore storytelling pleasure cruise that tours the lake in a large green sea-serpent-shaped pontoon boat. In June of 2002—the height of tourist season—the monster boat had its own run-in with the real Bear Lake Monster. The boat's owner reported that a green beast with red eyes swam under the vessel and lifted it a few feet on its humped back before swimming away. To quote the late, great Jack Palance, "Believe it … or not."

The Flathead Lake Monster

CHARACTERISTICS: Smooth black skin

SIZE: Ten to sixty feet long

HABITAT: Flathead Lake, Montana

APPETITE: Probably fish

Originally spotted in 1889 by passengers aboard the steamer *U.S. Grant,* the Flathead Lake Monster is described, as many lake monsters are, as being a dark snake or eel-shaped creature that moves through the water in an undulating motion and often appears as multiple humps protruding from the water. The beast has been seen by fishermen, locals and tourists ever since. The Flathead Lake Monster has never shown any aggressive behavior and rarely bothers anyone—aside from chewing holes in fishing nets from time to time.

Jackalope

CHARACTERISTICS: Resembles a rabbit or hare almost exactly, save for deer or elk-like antlers protruding from its head; its milk is said to have medicinal properties and is also a reported aphrodisiac

---

SIZE: Usually three to four feet tall if you include the antlers; weighs ten to fifteen pounds

---

HABITAT: Western states, particularly Wyoming

APPETITE: An affinity for alcohol (whiskey in particular), which may be used to tempt them into capture (alcohol tends to slow the animals, making them easier to hunt)

PRECAUTIONS: Jackalopes are very aggressive and use their antlers to gore their enemies, much like bulls. They should be approached with extreme caution.

Also known as deer-bunnies or warrior rabbits, Jackalopes are one of the most common folklore monsters that populate the United States. Nearly everyone is familiar with the Jackalope and has seen a stuffed one (most likely a fake produced through creative taxidermy, as Jackalopes are a very tricky species). Known to inhabit western states, Jackalopes have been witnessed since the first settlers began westward expansion and have been the subject of wild hunting stories, campfire tales and truck stop jokes ever since.

Despite their disarming resemblance to a typical rabbit or hare, Jackalopes are aggressive and mischievous animals and can be dangerous if encountered. Jackalopes are reported to have the ability to mimic the human voice, and legend has it that in the Old West they used to taunt cowboys as they sang around campfires—the Jackalope would occasionally sing back.

For skeptics, Jackalope sightings may possibly be explained by the fact that rabbits and hares occasionally contract a disease caused by a virus that causes them to grow horn-like growths on their heads. The virus is similar to one that causes genital warts in humans.

Whether real or fake, Jackalopes are one of the most easily researchable and common of all the North American monsters and are a perfect starting point for the amateur monster spotter.

The Pend Oreille Paddler

This plesiosaur-like creature inhabits Lake Pend Oreille, Idaho. Seen since the 1940s, the creature is said to have attacked a young girl at Sandpoint City Beach in 1977. The creature was named the Pend Oreille Paddler in a tabloid article about the attack. The article's accompanying photograph turned out to be of a giant papier-mâché catfish from a local play.

Penelope

CHARACTERISTICS: Tangled hair, fearsome claws and fangs

SIZE: Six to seven feet tall

HABITAT: The Sierra Nevada Mountains

APPETITE: Raw flesh

PRECAUTIONS: Penelope is a reputed man-eater fond of disemboweling her victims.

Once human, this terrifying creature is the product of a terrible tragedy. Legend has it that Penelope is a woman who was mutated by toxic waste. In the aftermath of an automobile accident that claimed the life of her husband, Penelope wandered into the woods and became lost. Seeking shelter from the winter cold, she crawled inside a contaminated metal barrel. Relying on a diet of uncooked forest animals that she killed with her bare hands, she was slowly transformed by the radioactive materials in her makeshift home. Her grief, combined with her exposure to the toxins, made her into a vicious hairy beast with a taste for human flesh. Penelope is said to have claimed the lives of several campers and forest rangers.

 ## Shunka Warakin

CHARACTERISTICS: A wolflike animal with a hunched back and a long snout

---

SIZE: Three to four feet tall at the shoulder

HABITAT: The Great Plains of the United States

APPETITE: Carnivorous

Shunka Warakin, or Shunka Warak'in, is a Native American term meaning "carries off dogs." During the pioneer days, Indian tribes as well as white setters told of a large canine that roamed the Great Plains. The creature was said to resemble a cross between a wolf and a hyena or wild boar with a long muzzle. Shunka Warakin is believed by many cryptozoologists to have been a prehistoric species of hyena indigenous to North America. The beast is now believed to be extinct, though in the early 1900s a specimen was reportedly shot, mounted and displayed in a general

store/museum in Henry's Lake, Idaho. The owner gave it the name "Ringdocus."

Some believe that Shunka Warakin still roams the country and is responsible for a number of supposed monster sightings. Werewolf and Chupacabra sightings have both been explained by the possibility of the existence of such a creature.

Slimy Slim

> **CHARACTERISTICS:** Lake serpent with brownish-green mottled skin and a cow-like head, with a stubby nose
>
> ---
>
> **SIZE:** Twenty to fifty feet long
>
> ---
>
> **HABITAT:** Payette Lake, Idaho
>
> ---
>
> **APPETITE:** Unknown

This long-necked, flat-headed lake serpent reportedly resides in Idaho's Payette Lake. There were a number of sightings during the 1930s and 1940s, which led a local newspaper to hold a contest to find a name for the creature. The winning entry was actually "Sharlie," after the catchphrase of the popular radio character Detective Baron Munchausen, who would say, "Vas you dere, Sharlie?" Locals still refer to the creature as Sharlie, while others have taken to calling the beast Slimy Slim.

Monsters of the Southwest

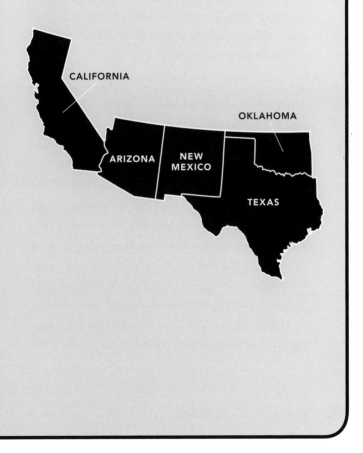

CALIFORNIA

OKLAHOMA

ARIZONA

NEW MEXICO

TEXAS

✦ Big Bird

> **CHARACTERISTICS:** Long-tailed winged creature with very smooth dark feathers (or possibly no feathers at all); also has a very thin beak that is in some cases described as transparent
>
> ---
>
> **SIZE:** Four to eight feet tall, with an eight- to fifteen-foot wingspan
>
> ---
>
> **HABITAT:** South Texas
>
> ---
>
> **APPETITE:** Carnivorous
>
> ---
>
> **PRECAUTIONS:** The creature seems to have no fear of humans, dogs, or even guns, and attacks indiscriminately at night.

A large flying menace known as Big Bird has terrorized south Texas since the 1940s. Not to be confused with the tall, lumbering *Sesame Street* character, Texas's Big Bird is a huge winged mystery creature that swoops down upon men and livestock under the cover of darkness. During 1976, there were a large number of reports of Big Bird attacks in Brownsville, Texas. The creature was described as flying with an effortless gliding motion. No one ever reported seeing the flapping of wings—a detail that has led many to speculate that Big Bird is extraterrestrial in nature.

Reports of Big Bird have been linked to a Texas legend about a witch known as La Lechuza, who transforms herself into a large owl at night. Descriptions of the creature also bear a striking resemblance to legends of the Thunderbird.

See also *La Lechuza,* page 130; *Thunderbird,* page 136.

The Cactus Cat

CHARACTERISTICS: Feline with porcupine-like quills covering its body; a branched tail; sharp spurs on its front legs

------

SIZE: Approximately two feet long

HABITAT: Southwestern United States

APPETITE: Fermented cactus sap

PRECAUTIONS: The cactus cat is a lousy drunk and may be dangerous when intoxicated.

This nocturnal desert creature is renowned for giving cowboys a hard time. The spiny beast uses its sharp appendages to slice open cacti and returns later to lap up the fermented sap. The Cactus Cat then becomes intoxicated and is a notoriously loud drunk. The creature spends the rest of the night yowling as it runs sporadically through the desert slashing cacti and whatever else is in its path.

 ## The Elmendorf Creature

CHARACTERISTICS: Short, bluish-grey, doglike creature with a mottled appearance and a toothy overbite

---

SIZE: Two to three feet long, weighing approximately twenty pounds

---

HABITAT: Southern Texas

APPETITE: Carnivorous, often preys upon livestock

PRECAUTIONS: These animals have ferocious appetites—in one instance, one slaughtered more than thirty chickens in an afternoon.

The Elmendorf Creature is an unidentified species of canine that was discovered in Elmendorf, Texas, in August 2004 when a rancher shot a strange hairless beast that was devouring his chickens. The animal was unidentifiable—theories ranged from the beast being a mangy coyote to a deformed deer. Other sightings followed and an identical creature was shot in Lufkin, Texas. DNA testing was performed, and it was determined that the creatures were some sort of canine, but beyond that, the results were inconclusive.

Pictures of the Elmendorf specimens have been widely circulated on the Internet and many believe that the creatures are actually Chupacabras—creatures known to drain the blood from goats and other livestock in a vampire-like manner. Chupacabra sightings originated in Mexico during the 1990s and migrated across the southwestern United States, leaving a wake of slaughtered livestock. News of the Chupacabra spread on the Internet like wildfire and, with the help of the Elmendorf photos, the beast quickly became a pop culture icon.

See also *El Chupacabra,* page 183.

Elsie

CHARACTERISTICS: Snaky and dragon-like, exhibiting humps

SIZE: From twelve feet to one hundred feet long

HABITAT: Lake Elsinore, CA

APPETITE: Omnivorous

PRECAUTIONS: As with many lake monsters, there are no specific examples of Elsie being a threat to humans, but caution is advised when engaging in aquatic recreation in the waters of Lake Elsinore.

Elsie is a humped serpentine creature said to live in southern California's Lake Elsinore. The monster has been the subject of sightings and local stories since the late 1800s. Reports range from wild tales of a one hundred-foot long dragon-like beast to more modest accounts of a twelve-foot long plesiosaur-like creature. Sightings have persisted to this day despite the fact that the lake dried up completely in 1954 and no monster was found.

The Giant Freshwater Octopus

CHARACTERISTICS: Reddish brown with leathery skin

SIZE: Over twenty feet long

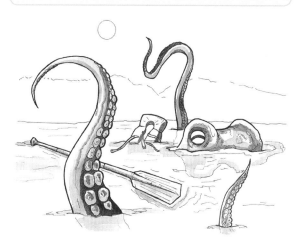

Lakes in Oklahoma rate high in instances of drowning. Some believe that drowning victims actually fall prey to the giant octopi living in the lakes. Several of Oklahoma's lakes, including Lake Thunderbird, Lake Oologah and Lake Tenkiller, are said to be home to these monstrous creatures that are thought to be responsible for dragging swimmers and fishermen to their watery deaths.

The Hawley Him

CHARACTERISTICS: Tall, hairy humanoid

SIZE: Six to seven feet tall

HABITAT: Areas surrounding Hawley, Texas	
APPETITE: Omnivorous	
PRECAUTIONS: Can be aggressive, has been known to throw sticks and stones	

Eastern Texas has its share of Bigfoot-type creature sightings. One such beast is known as the Hawley Him. It is described as a tall ape-man with long arms. The Hawley Him was first sighted in July of 1977 when two boys clearing brush at a ranch heard breaking tree limbs and were assaulted by the monster as it threw rocks at them. They fled the scene and returned with a neighbor armed with a rifle. All three witnesses saw the creature, which they fired upon and apparently missed. They claimed it left behind large footprints and a foul rotting smell, the presence of which probably links the creature to a group of monsters known as Skunk Apes.

See also *Skunk Ape,* page 75.

 ## Hodgee

CHARACTERISTICS: Long neck, flippers	
SIZE: Approximately twenty feet long	
HABITAT: Lake Hodges, San Diego, California	
APPETITE: Fish and live sea lions (when made available)	

This lake serpent is said to inhabit Lake Hodges near San Diego, California. A typical plesiosaur-looking monster, the most notable detail about Hodgee is an elaborate capture attempt made in the 1930s involving a steel cage and a live sea lion. A camera encased in glass and attached to a nearby buoy was used to capture a photograph of a dark shape in the water with apparent flippers. The sea lion disappeared and public outcry over the use of the poor animal as bait resulted in the project's demise.

The Hoop Snake

CHARACTERISTICS: When moving, this long snake resembles a bicycle tire rolling along

SIZE: Ten to fifteen feet long

HABITAT: Southwestern United States

APPETITE: Small desert animals

PRECAUTIONS: The hoop snake's venom is almost always lethal.

The Hoop Snake resembles an ordinary black snake but moves in a peculiar manner. When chasing its prey, the creature grabs its own tail in its mouth and moves in a rolling motion, like a wheel. The snake is able to move very quickly in this manner and is quite venomous. Anyone being chased by a Hoop Snake is advised to jump through the center of its hoop, which can confuse it long enough to possibly escape.

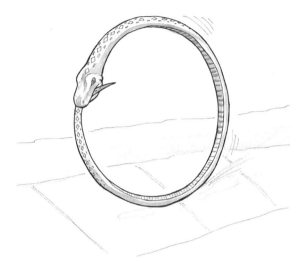

La Lechuza

CHARACTERISTICS: Resembles a large owl, or in some cases, an eagle

---

SIZE: Reports vary

HABITAT: South Texas

APPETITE: Unknown

PRECAUTIONS: Be advised: La Lechuza has the ability to render your automobile's electrical system useless.

Southern Texas seems to be a hotbed of activity for flying monsters, including Big Bird, Thunderbird and El Chupacabra sightings. One interesting legend centers on witches who are capable of transforming themselves into owl-like birds known as Lechuzas. These creatures are sinister visitors who often swoop down on folks traveling in automobiles and wreak havoc with the cars' electrical systems. When cars mysteriously die, headlights fail and windshield wipers come on for no apparent reason, many Texans believe La Lechuza is afoot.

Some legends say that Lechuzas are spirits of women who were wronged by a faithless husband. Due to their supernatural nature, there are a few ways to guard oneself against La Lechuza. A rope or string with seven knots serves as a talisman against the creature. The services of a curandera—a Mexican shaman who practices ancient Mayan healing techniques—may help.

Prayer is also said to work. If all else fails, shotguns seem to be effective against the creatures—though after blasting a bird out of the sky only to have it transform into the body of a woman, you'll probably have some serious explaining to do.

The Lake Worth Monster

CHARACTERISTICS: Humanoid torso with the legs of a goat; covered in white fur and scales

---

SIZE: Six to seven feet tall, weighing approximately three hundred pounds

---

HABITAT: Areas surrounding Lake Worth in Fort Worth, Texas

APPETITE: Carnivorous—typically eats pets and livestock; also seems fond of fried chicken

---

PRECAUTIONS: Very powerful and dangerous; known to be able to hurl heavy items such as tires; has a vicious appetite

During the summer of 1969, Texas' Lake Worth area was terrorized by a strange satyr-like creature known simply as the Lake Worth Monster. Described by the *Fort Worth Star Telegram* as being a "fishy man-goat," this beast has the legs of a goat and the upper body of a Sasquatch or ape. It is covered in white fur and has scaly skin around its eyes.

The monster was seen by hundreds of people during that fateful summer, and reportedly jumped on the hoods of cars, flung an automobile tire toward a group of about thirty startled witnesses, and devoured several sheep. The monster even attacked a man camped by the lake who survived the encounter by giving the beast a bag of leftover chicken, which it stuffed into its mouth before leaping into the lake and swimming away. People were genuinely frightened and the local police conducted a serious investiga-

tion. They even sighted and fired upon the creature, which left behind a blood trail—but eventually the beast eluded them.

While not an aquatic animal, the Lake Worth Monster is an excellent swimmer, and several witnesses have seen the beast swimming to and from Greer Island, where many believe it lives.

The Monster of Elizabeth Lake

CHARACTERISTICS: Demonic-looking creature with leathery gargoyle-like bat wings

SIZE: More than six feet tall

HABITAT: Elizabeth Lake, California

APPETITE: Unknown

PRECAUTIONS: Folklore associates this monstrosity with Satan himself. As with any off the devil's minions, the Monster of Elizabeth Lake should be considered demonic and evil.

First spotted in the 1830s by Mexican ranchers, this bat-winged, griffin-like monster is said to dwell in California's Elizabeth Lake. According to legend, the lake was created by the devil, and the beast is one of his pets.

One-Eye

A giant serpent said to live in Lake Granbury in Granbury, Texas. Early Spanish traders told of the creature and Native Americans made animal sacrifices to appease the monster.

Tahoe Tessie

CHARACTERISTICS: Dark-colored serpentine body

SIZE: Twenty to sixty feet long

HABITAT: Lake Tahoe, California

APPETITE: Fish

Tahoe Tessie, or simply Tessie, is a reptilian creature that is said to live in the depths of Lake Tahoe on the California–Nevada border. The lake is roughly twenty-two miles long and twelve miles wide and reaches depths of over sixteen hundred feet—definitely capable of hiding such a monster. Reports of Tessie date back to the Washoe Indians, who told of monsters in the lake. Sightings continue to this day and are quite frequent. Witnesses rarely see more than several humps moving through the water in an undulating motion. The reports are usually so un-dramatic that they somehow seem more credible.

In the mid 1970s, famed oceanographer Jacques Cousteau led an expedition into Lake Tahoe's depths.

Whatever he found he refused to divulge, reportedly stating, "The world isn't ready for what was down there." Many believe he had a frightening encounter with Tessie. Some locals theorize that Cousteau may have encountered a grisly underwater graveyard for pinstriped gangsters of the 1920s and 1930s, as an area off of the lake's south shore is said to have been a favorite dumping ground for mafia killers back in the day. Extreme depths and cold water tend to prevent corpses from bloating and rising to the surface.

Thunderbird

CHARACTERISTICS: Reports vary—some describe a large condor-like bird, and in other instances they tell of a prehistoric pterodactyl-like creature.

SIZE: Fifteen- to thirty-five-foot wingspan

HABITAT: Southwestern and midwestern
United States

APPETITE: Carnivorous

PRECAUTIONS: Known to try to carry off livestock,
pets and children

Almost every Native American tribe tells of a legendary Thunderbird. In most cases, the creature is a large bird with huge wings that it can beat together to create thunder. Lightning shoots from the Thunderbird's eyes, its shadow blocks out the sun and wherever it goes, storms tend to follow. The Thunderbird of legend is so large that entire lakes may form on its shoulders, and on occasion it flies over oceans to prey upon whales.

Myth? Most likely. But as with many myths, the legend of the Thunderbird may have a basis in reality. The large vulture-like California condor has a nine-foot wingspan, and its South American cousin the Andean condor is the largest known bird in the world with a wingspan that can reach as much as twelve feet. While these large birds inhabit specific regions, cryptozoologists believe there may be a related species that still makes occasional appearances throughout North America, particularly in the Southwest.

In many instances, descriptions of large birds with wingspans of twenty to thirty feet match the description of the Andean condor, which is black with a white

ring around its neck. Birds fitting this description have been spotted flying through the skies, attacking children and livestock, and terrorizing trailer parks throughout North America, from Arizona to Texas to Missouri to Illinois—definitely outside of the Andean condor's normal territory.

In 1977, a ten-year-old boy from Lawndale, Illinois, was carried several feet when one of two Thunderbirds swooped down and tried to abduct him. Several witnesses—including the boy's mother, whose screams frightened the beast away—claimed that the large black birds had ten-foot wingspans and white neck feathers. Reports of these large birds continued in the Lawndale area for several months.

Some cryptozoologists believe these Thunderbirds could be related to a prehistoric condor-like bird species known as Teratorns, fossils of which have been found in Nevada and California.

Other Thunderbird reports tell of a different type of creature—an alligator-faced flying creature with featherless bat wings. One such beast is said to have been shot by a couple of cowboys in Tombstone, Arizona, in the late 1800s. They pinned the beast to the side of a barn by its wings, which spanned the barn's entire length. Photographs of the event are said to have appeared in the *Tombstone Epitaph*. Sadly, all records of the photos seem to have vanished.

Whether a relative of the Andean condor or some strange pterosaur, the fact is that a large mystery creature haunts the skies of the United States and may offer scientists a chance to discover a believed extinct species and monster enthusiasts the opportunity to witness a living myth. For those interested in trying to catch a glimpse of a Thunderbird, the Ohio River Valley from the Ozarks to the Appalachian Mountains is reported to be a migration pattern for large birds matching this description.

See also *Big Bird,* page 122.

Monsters of the Pacific Northwest

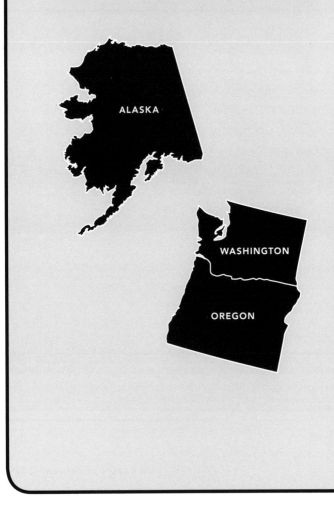

ALASKA

WASHINGTON

OREGON

The Akhlut

> **CHARACTERISTICS:** Shape-shifting killer whale that can change into a wolf
> -------
> **SIZE:** Alternately wolf- or whale-sized
> -------
> **HABITAT:** Alaskan Coast along the Bering Sea
> -------
> **APPETITE:** Eats human flesh
> -------
> **PRECAUTIONS:** See above

The Akhlut is a supernatural killer whale from Inuit folklore that is capable of assuming the shape of a wolf in order to hunt for humans on land. A telltale sign that an Akhlut is afoot are wolf tracks that lead to and from the edge of the ice. The beast is probably nearby waiting to emerge from the ocean and attack.

The Amhuluk

> **CHARACTERISTICS:** Serpentine with horns
> -------
> **SIZE:** Most likely similar to other lake serpents, anywhere from thirty to one hundred feet long
> -------
> **HABITAT:** Lakes surrounding Forkend Mountain in Oregon
> -------
> **APPETITE:** Unknown

The Amhuluk are monsters said to inhabit an enchanted lake of the same name near Forked Mountain, Oregon. The serpents are said to try to lure humans, particularly children, into the water to drown them and transform them into monsters as well.

One legend of the Amhuluk tells of three children playing near the water. The beast impaled the children with its horns and dragged them into the lake. The father came looking for the children and their bodies rose from the lake mud as the undead. For five days, the man conversed with the ghostly remains of his children, imploring them to return to him. The children could not and were pulled back into the lake by Amhuluk, presumably to be transformed into monsters themselves.

The Amikuk

CHARACTERISTICS: Varies—according to some descriptions, has a slimy pelt with humanoid appendages; some accounts tell of a serpentine creature and still other accounts tell of an invisible beast

SIZE: Unspecified—but definitely large

HABITAT: Originates at the Alaskan Coast along the Bering Sea; has the ability to travel considerable distances inland

APPETITE: Occasionally preys upon humans

PRECAUTIONS: This creature is difficult to escape. If you observe the beast in the water, do not presume that you are safe on land. Take measures to distance yourself from it and be prepared to perform evasive maneuvers.

The Amikuk is a monster from Inuit folklore that has the ability to swim though the tundra, actually diving in and out of the earth as if it were water. In some traditions, the creature normally inhabits the sea but travels through land to prey upon humans. Other legends speak of the nest of an Amikuk, which can multiply riches—when something is placed into the nest, the next day you will find it has increased in size or quantity.

Antukai

CHARACTERISTICS: Otter-like

SIZE: Grizzly bear-sized

HABITAT: Lakes surrounding Forkend Mountain in Oregon

APPETITE: Unknown

According to legend, this otter-like monstrosity was once a grizzly bear but was transformed after being lured into an enchanted lake by the serpent Amhuluk.

Asin

CHARACTERISTICS: Humanoid

SIZE: Ranges in height from a little girl to a woman

HABITAT: Pacific Northwest

APPETITE: Human flesh

PRECAUTIONS: Like many spirits of the woods, Asin is capable of magic and trickery—it is best to avoid any forest you suspect she inhabits.

The Alsea tribe told of a cannibalistic girl named Asin who lived in the woods along the coast in the Pacific Northwest. She will claim anyone who wanders into the forest as her victim but is particularly fond of luring children to follow her. Asin's laughter is an omen of impending death and to dream of her is a portent of disaster.

Batsquatch

CHARACTERISTICS: Dark skin with a purple tinge, wings like those of a pterodactyl; appears to be a cross between an ape and a bat

---

SIZE: Four to six feet tall

HABITAT: Areas surrounding Mount St. Helens and Mount Rainier in Washington

---

APPETITE: Unknown

PRECAUTIONS: May pose a threat to livestock, pets and small children

Batsquatch is the name given to a large, primarily nocturnal bat-like creature reported to live in the state of Washington. Descriptions of the beast with its simian features, purple skin and large bat wings call to mind the visage of the infamous flying monkeys from *The Wizard of Oz*. While the name Batsquatch is obviously derived from the term Sasquatch, there is no reason to believe the animal has anything to do with Bigfoot lore.

Not much is known about Batsquatch other than its terrifying appearance. It has been suggested that the creature may be responsible for the disappearance of livestock such as chickens, goats and the occasional cow. In 1994, one of these monsters was even caught on camera by a local mountain climber/liquor store owner named Butch Whittaker when he spotted the beast as he was prepping for a climb, though many consider the photographs to be a hoax.

 ## Bigfoot

CHARACTERISTICS: Tall, hairy, apelike humanoid with large five-toed feet

---

SIZE: Approximately six to ten feet tall, weighing two hundred to five hundred pounds

---

HABITAT: Pacific Northwest and Canada

APPETITE: Omnivore

PRECAUTIONS: May be prone to kidnapping humans, with the intention of mating with them.

Bigfoot is more than a monster. The beast is a pop culture icon. Without a doubt the most famous monster in North America, perhaps the world, Bigfoot's name has been used commercially on everything from amusement park rides to thirty-two-ounce gas station fountain drinks to pizza—anything presented as a gargantuan size or value. And it's easy to understand why. By all accounts, Bigfoot is the closest thing we have to a modern-day giant—a ten-foot-tall hairy man-beast with footprints measuring up to sixteen inches long and seventeen inches wide.

Bigfoot's home is widely accepted as being in the Pacific Northwest and parts of Canada. While apelike creatures have been sighted all over the United States, there are significant differences that suggest that while they may be related, the hairy hominids living in different areas of the country are not necessarily Bigfoot creatures. Bigfoot is typically thought to be the same as the Sasquatch (a Canadian term derived from several Native American words for the creatures).

While sightings of creatures matching Bigfoot's description have been reported since the late eighteenth century, the term Bigfoot first became recognized in 1958 when a northern California construction worker named Jerry Crew showed a plaster cast of a large

footprint he had found in the Bluff Creek Valley to an area newspaper. The resulting article referred to the creature creating the prints as "Bigfoot," and the name stuck.

While often thought of as shy and even gentle, Bigfoot creatures have been known to kidnap people, usually with the apparent intention of mating with them or inducting them into their society. They typically treat human captives kindly and only show hostility when they attempt to escape. In 1924, a Bigfoot abducted a British Columbian prospector from his campsite. The creature scooped up Albert Ostman in his sleeping bag and carried him in the makeshift sack for a considerable distance. When the sleeping bag was opened, Ostman found himself amongst an entire Bigfoot family. He was kept for several days before he managed to escape.

A wealth of Bigfoot evidence has been collected since the late 1950s including plaster casts of footprints, hair and feces samples, and recordings of the creatures' calls. The most amazing piece of evidence is the famous Patterson-Gimlin film, shot on October 20, 1967, by Bigfoot enthusiasts Roger Patterson and Bob Gimlin, which captures on 16mm film a live female Bigfoot in the act of lumbering along the edge of the woods. Interestingly, the footage was filmed near Bluff Creek—the same location of the first plaster casts collected by Jerry Crew. To this day, the film is the subject of much controversy and speculation.

Encounters with Bigfoot typically occur in wooded areas or driving along desolate roads in the late evening, night or at dawn, as the creatures seem to be primarily nocturnal. Most Bigfoot encounters portray the animals as shy and docile, but there have been instances where they have been incited to violence. One Bigfoot attack in 1924 involving a group of miners occurred in a canyon near Mount St. Helens. One of the miners apparently shot and wounded a Bigfoot and invoked the wrath of the Bigfoot's tribe. Once the sun went down, the men found themselves under siege as several shrieking hairy ape-men hurled sticks and stones at their cabin all night long. The canyon, a hot spot for Bigfoot sightings, was known as Ape Canyon until it was unfortunately filled in with mud by the eruption of Mount St. Helens in 1980.

Despite the harrowing tales of kidnappings and occasional attacks, Bigfoot creatures probably have much more to fear from humans than we do from them. Human encroachment on their natural habitat has most likely driven the Bigfoot population to near extinction.

No matter the status of Bigfoot's current population, no one can deny the creature's existence in our culture. Bigfoot is the subject of movies such as *Harry and the Hendersons* (1987), and has made numerous appearances in television shows, including *The Six Million Dollar Man* of the 1970s in which the creature was brilliantly portrayed as the guardian of a group of visiting space aliens. Plus, one can easily argue that the creature was most likely the inspiration for *Star Wars'* Chewbacca.

So ... the big question. Is Bigfoot real? With a character that is so much larger than life, that has such a grip on the imagination and our primal fears, my question to you is, does the fact of whether the creature really exists even matter? The phenomenon itself exists. The beast's notoriety is undeniable. The evidence has been collected and cross-examined countless times and never disproved. Of course, you can be scientific about it and wait for absolute, undeniable proof. But isn't it more fun to believe in something? Do you really want to question the existence of the Santa Claus of the monster world? Bigfoot is real.

Colossal Claude

CHARACTERISTICS: Snaky body with a camel-like head; gray in color; sometimes described as having fur

----

SIZE: Approximately forty feet long

HABITAT: Columbia River, Oregon, and the Oregon Coast

APPETITE: Fish

Colossal Claude is the moniker given to a sea monster reported to inhabit the Pacific Ocean along the Oregon Coast. First spotted near the mouth of the Columbia River, which borders Oregon and Washington State, Claude has been seen by sailors since the 1930s. Proximity and description suggest that sightings of Colossal Claude may be linked to the Cadborosaurus sightings of British Columbia.

See also *Cadborosaurus,* page 162.

Gumberoo

> **CHARACTERISTICS:** Resembles a large hairless bear; has very thick skin
>
> -------
>
> **SIZE:** Anywhere from four to six feet tall
>
> -------
>
> **HABITAT:** Pacific Northwest
>
> -------
>
> **APPETITE:** Carnivore
>
> -------
>
> **PRECAUTIONS:** Will explode if exposed to flame

The Gumberoo is a strange bearlike creature with rubbery or leathery skin that is impervious to gunfire. The creatures can be vicious and should be avoided.

It is said that the only way to defeat a Gumberoo is with fire, though doing so is very dangerous because it causes the beast to explode.

The Iliamna Lake Monsters

CHARACTERISTICS: Gray or silvery in color (sometimes with black stripes down their sides)

SIZE: Up to thirty feet long

HABITAT: Lake Iliamna, Alaska

APPETITE: Fish and the occasional human victim

PRECAUTIONS: These vicious barracuda-like fish have been known to attack boats.

Most lake monsters are believed to be single entities living within the confines of a lake—usually evolutionary throwbacks or survivors from prehistoric times. Alaska's Lake Iliamna boasts a different kind of monster. Since the early nineteenth century, people have witnessed a group of very large and aggressive fish living in the lake. Aleut Indians first told of the creatures that were said to attack canoes and devour braves. The monstrous fish are said to reach lengths of thirty feet and have blunt heads that they use to smash through the bottoms of boats and throw victims into the water. Iliamna's big fish are said to resemble large barracuda and have been seen by countless fishermen and Alaskan bush pilots

who have sighted schools of them swimming throughout the lake. They are so large that they are at times mistaken for inland whales, but unlike whales they have vertical tails. The large population of these creatures lends credence to their possible existence, suggesting they may be an undiscovered species. Some theorize that they are a breed of freshwater sharks.

The Kushtaka

CHARACTERISTICS: Can assume the form of an otter or a human

SIZE: Varies depending on how the Kushtaka manifests itself

HABITAT: Southeastern Alaska

APPETITE: Unknown

PRECAUTIONS: While they can at times seem friendly or helpful, you should never trust a Kushtaka, or you may become one yourself!

The Kushtaka are shape-shifters from Tlingit Indian legend that can transform themselves from humans into otters. Stories about the intentions of the Kushtaka vary—in some accounts, the creatures are wicked and enjoy tricking sailors, often leading them to their deaths. In other tales, they may save a lost person from freezing to death by transforming him into a fellow Kushtaka. They also are said to spirit away human babies with the intention of creating more Kushtakas.

Sasquatch

CHARACTERISTICS: Tall, hairy, apelike humanoid with large five-toed feet

----

SIZE: Approximately six to ten feet tall

HABITAT: Pacific Northwest and Canada

APPETITE: Omnivore

PRECAUTIONS: Normally thought of as shy and docile but may be incited to violence if provoked—also have been known to kidnap humans on occasion.

Sasquatch is a term that was invented by Canadian journalist J.W. Burns in the 1920s to describe a group of hairy giants of several Native American legends. The word is derived from various similar-sounding Native American names.

Most consider Sasquatch and Bigfoot to be the same creature—a hairy, apelike, bipedal man-beast living in the Pacific Northwest and parts of Canada. Others contend that there are differences, portraying Bigfoot as a solitary creature and Sasquatch as a social animal that lives with a family or tribe.

According to most legends and accounts Sasquatch is a relatively benign being—a gentle woodland giant that subsists mostly by eating vegetation and berries. There are some accounts in which the creatures abduct humans, but even when they do they usually treat their captives kindly, apparently wanting to induct them into their family or tribe—or possibly mate with them. There are accounts of attacks by creatures thought to be Sasquatch, but they are far outnumbered by encounters of a more amiable nature.

See also *Bigfoot,* page 146.

The Tirisuk

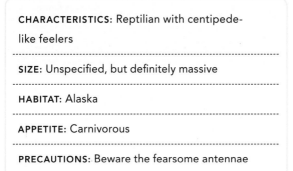

CHARACTERISTICS: Reptilian with centipede-like feelers

SIZE: Unspecified, but definitely massive

HABITAT: Alaska

APPETITE: Carnivorous

PRECAUTIONS: Beware the fearsome antennae

The Tirisuk are large beasts of Inuit legend that resemble a cross between reptiles and insects with huge snapping-turtle-like jaws and long antennae that they use to capture their prey.

The Wallowa Lake Monster

CHARACTERISTICS: Descriptions vary

SIZE: Fifty to one hundred feet long

HABITAT: Wallowa Lake, Oregon

APPETITE: Unknown

Wallowa Lake in Oregon is said to be home to a strange aquatic monster that has been described as having the combined features of a hog, buffalo or rhinoceros with those of a shark. Sightings of the Wallowa Lake Monster date back to Native American legends—the Nez Perce tribe tells of a gigantic horned beast that originally lived in the mountains but was chased into the lake by a young brave who wanted to claim the beast as a trophy but was subsequently pulled into the depths by the creature.

Modern reports seem to agree that the creature, sometimes referred to as "Wally," has seven humps along its spine that protrude from the water.

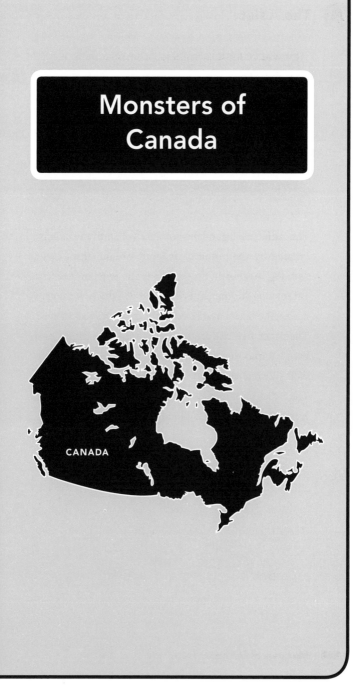

Monsters of Canada

CANADA

The Adlet

CHARACTERISTICS: Half dog, half human with reddish hair

SIZE: Six to seven feet tall

HABITAT: Arctic regions—particularly the shores of Hudson Bay

APPETITE: Human blood

The Adlet are legendary creatures of Inuit mythology, created by the union of an Inuit woman and a large red dog. According to the story, the woman bore ten infant dog-human hybrids, five of which were sent across the ocean and sired the European races of men. The other five children were incredibly vicious, and escaped into the wild, where they bred a race of werewolf-like monsters that came to be known as the Adlet. The Adlet hunt in packs and are fond of dismembering humans to drink their blood.

The Amarok

A giant supernatural wolf of Canadian folklore.

See also *Waheela,* page 178.

Bokwus

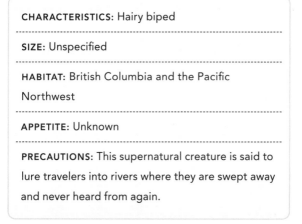

CHARACTERISTICS: Hairy biped

SIZE: Unspecified

HABITAT: British Columbia and the Pacific Northwest

APPETITE: Unknown

PRECAUTIONS: This supernatural creature is said to lure travelers into rivers where they are swept away and never heard from again.

The Kwakiutl tribe of Canada tell of a wild man or spirit of the woods known as Bokwus, who leads the spirits of people who have drowned to his invisible home in the forest. A malevolent version of the legend says that Bokwus lures travelers to watery deaths and collects their drowned souls, and often tries to tempt humans to eat "ghost food" in order to make them like himself. Bokwus inhabits the tree-lined edges of rivers.

The legend of Bokwus seems to have much in common with Canadian Wendigo lore. Description and location also suggest that this creature may be related to Bigfoot and Sasquatch phenomena.

See also *Wendigo, page 179; Bigfoot, page 146;* and *Sasquatch, page 155.*

Cadborosaurus

CHARACTERISTICS: Serpentine body that appears in coils or humps; also has flippers, a horse- or camel-like head, and a fluke-like tail

----

SIZE: Fifteen to fifty feet long

HABITAT: Cadboro Bay, off of British Columbia, and along the coast of the Pacific Northwest

----

APPETITE: Fish and seaweed, most likely

In the 1930s, a British Columbia newspaper editor held a contest to name a sea serpent seen regularly in the Cadboro Bay area off of British Columbia near Vancouver Island. The winning entry was Cadborosaurus, as the creature came to be known—or Caddy for short.

Caddy has much in common with another British Columbia monster, Ogopogo—an inland serpent in Lake Okanagan. The beast resembles a large snake or eel with flippers and a head like a horse.

Scientists have had some near misses for attaining tangible evidence of Caddy. In 1937, the rotting carcass of a Cadborosaurus was extracted from the stomach of a sperm whale and was taken to a Naden Harbour whaling station where several photographs were taken. Unfortunately, the body was disposed of before any conclusive examination could be performed. Then in 1968, a fisherman caught a live baby Cadborosaurus and intended to deliver the specimen to scientists once he reached land; however, he was forced to release the creature because he feared it might injure or kill itself trying to escape.

Despite the lack of an actual Cadborosaurus specimen, the sheer wealth of sightings lend credibility to the possibility of the creature's existence.

Cressie

> **CHARACTERISTICS:** Snakelike or eel-like body
>
> ------
>
> **SIZE:** Fifteen to twenty feet long
>
> ------
>
> **HABITAT:** Crescent Lake, Newfoundland
>
> ------
>
> **APPETITE:** Carnivorous

Cressie is the name given to a creature—or more likely a group of creatures—seen in Newfoundland's Crescent Lake. The animals are said to resemble an eel of gigantic proportion, having a snake-like body and the head of a fish. Cressie has been seen since the early 1900s and is thought to be quite vicious. In the mid-1980s, during the search for a body from a downed aircraft, a pair of scuba divers was attacked by a school of possible Cressies.

Descriptions of the creature have led many to believe that folks are simply seeing large eels. Crescent

Lake is indeed home to a large population of freshwater eels known as *Anguilloidei*, which typically can reach sizes of three to five feet in length.

 ## Gougou

> **CHARACTERISTICS:** Gigantic woman with fish scales
>
> --
>
> **SIZE:** Approximately fifty feet tall
>
> --
>
> **HABITAT:** A mysterious deserted island in the Gulf of Saint Lawrence
>
> --
>
> **APPETITE:** Carnivorous

Gougou is a giantess from the legends of the Micmac tribe of Native Americans. The story seems to have ties to legends of mermaids, only scarier. Gougou is said to wade through Canada's Gulf of Saint Lawrence, snatching fishermen from their boats and stuffing them into a leather pouch in order to devour them later back at her lair.

The Icegedunk

The Icegedunk is a strange creature from Canadian folklore that is said to resemble a seal with no flippers. This weird animal propels itself across land using a wheel-like appendage on its rear, and lives in British Columbia. Unfortunately, the Icegedunk is very rare and is on the verge of extinction.

Igopogo

CHARACTERISTICS: Snaky body with the head of a dog; gray in color; sometimes described as having flippers

----

SIZE: Fifteen to seventy feet long

HABITAT: Lake Simcoe, just north of Toronto

APPETITE: Fish

Igopogo, one of several monsters named for the famous Canadian lake monster Ogopogo, differs from other lake monsters in that it has a doglike head. The creature is described as relatively slow-moving and is fond of basking in the sun. Igopogo's habit of lingering near the lake surface leads many to believe that the beast is not a reptile but a mammal, similar to a giant seal.

Igopogo is also known by a couple of other local names depending on whom you ask—Beaverton Bessie along the eastern shore, and Kempenfelt Kelly near Kempenfelt Bay.

The Lake Utopia Monster

CHARACTERISTICS: Serpentine body with a very large head and mouth

---

SIZE: Thirty to fifty feet long

HABITAT: Lake Utopia, New Brunswick

APPETITE: Carnivorous

The Lake Utopia Monster is a gigantic eel-like beast with a large frightening mouth full of teeth—at least according to legend. Natives tell of a serpent in the lake that would attack their canoes, its gaping maw dripping with blood. White settlers described a vicious monster capable of smashing through layers of lake ice in the winter to snap its fearsome jaws at ice fishermen.

Modern reports of the creature portray a bit more docile lake serpent that lolls about, basking in the sun and diving beneath the water when encountered.

Manipogo

CHARACTERISTICS: Muddy brown or black serpentine body

SIZE: Anywhere from twelve to fifty feet long

HABITAT: Lakes Manitoba, Winnipeg, Winnipegosis, Dauphin, Cedar and Dirty, as well as connecting waterways

---

APPETITE: Fish, most likely

Manipogo is a name given to a population of lake monsters that seem to inhabit several connected lakes in Manitoba, Canada. The creature is named after the more famous Canadian lake monster Ogopogo and is sometimes referred to as Winnipogo by folks along the shores of Lake Winnipeg.

Manipogo is similar to other lake monsters in description. It is snake- or eel-like and gives the appearance of having humps as it moves through the water.

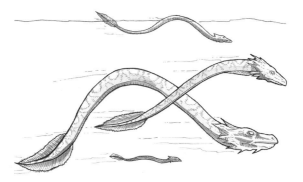

There are, however, a couple of interesting differences between Manipogo and other lake monsters. First, the creature rarely shows its head. Secondly, while most lake serpents are solitary animals, Manipogo seems to enjoy the company of others of its kind. Manipogos are often seen in groups of three or more, suggesting that the creatures may live in pods like whales. In the summer of 1960, a group of seventeen people reported seeing three of the creatures of varying sizes swimming together.

Manipogo has been the subject of a good deal of research. In the 1960s, two expeditions to search for the creature were organized by James McLeod, head of the Zoology Department at the University of Manitoba. He collected numerous reports of sightings and even a photograph of one of the animals taken by a tourist in 1962.

In 1997, an area farmer claimed to have shot a Manipogo. The claim coincided with a report of a sighting made by an officer of the Royal Canadian Mounted Police. The farmer was offering to sell the carcass to the first party willing to pay a sum of $200,000. The incident was investigated by renowned cryptozoologist Loren Coleman and the Ufology Research of Manitoba and was concluded to be a hoax.

Despite this unfortunate incident, there are a large number of credible eyewitness accounts that suggest that the system of lakes in Manitoba is home to something decidedly strange.

Mannegishi

> **CHARACTERISTICS:** Spindly, gray, hairless creatures with large noseless heads
>
> ---
>
> **SIZE:** Three to four feet tall
>
> ---
>
> **HABITAT:** Eastern Canada
>
> ---
>
> **APPETITE:** Unknown

Mannegishi are a legendary race of tricksters from Cree folklore. These lanky dwarfs are said to live in between rocks near rivers and like to play malicious tricks on people. Natives blamed the Mannegishi for upsetting canoes, sending braves into the rapids

to drown. The Iroquois tribe told a nearly identical legend and referred to the creature as Gahonga. Many speculate that witnesses saw a Mannegishi in Dover, Massachusetts, during the Dover Demon scare of the 1970s.

See also *The Dover Demon*, page 31.

Mussie

Mussie, also known as Hapyxelor, is the name given to a monster of various descriptions living in Muskrat Lake—a lake just northwest of Ottawa, Canada. According to early accounts, Mussie has three eyes, sharp teeth and a long tongue. More modern reports describe a large seal or walrus-like creature approximately twenty-five feet in length.

Ogopogo

CHARACTERISTICS: Dark blue, black or brown serpentine body with a white underbelly; flippers and serrations along the back

----

SIZE: Twenty to fifty feet long

HABITAT: Lake Okanagan, British Columbia

APPETITE: Fish and the occasional horse

Ogopogo has a long, dark undulating body that gives the appearance of humps protruding from the water. Its head is described as similar to that of a horse.

Sightings of Ogopogo date back to around 1860—approximately sixty years before reports of the Loch Ness Monster became so prevalent. Native Americans called the creature N'ha-a-itk or Naitaka, which means "snake-in-the-lake." Surprisingly, Ogopogo is not an Indian name at all. The name is a palindrome and actually was given by a visiting British entertainer named W.H. Brimblecombe, who was fascinated by the stories of the monster and wrote a goofy little song in which he names the creature Ogopogo. The song was performed at an area Rotary Club, and the name stuck.

Although many white settlers seemed to regard Ogopogo as simply an entertaining myth, Native American legends cast the creature in a different light. They

often flung sacrifices of small animals into the lake whenever crossing in a canoe to appease N'ha-a-itk and painted effigies of the monster on rocks near the water as warnings. According to legend, the creature lives in a cave under an area known as Squally Point near a small barren island in Lake Okanagan known as Rattlesnake Island. Braves who visited the island found it littered with the bones of N'ha-a-itk's victims—both animal and human.

Ogopogo seems to have a large appetite. In 1870, a man named John McDougal was swimming two horses across the lake behind his boat when suddenly the horses were pulled beneath the water and into the depths. There have been other reports of horses disappearing in this manner, as well as being pulled from the edge of the lake while drinking.

A very dramatic recent Ogopogo sighting was made in 2000 when cancer survivor Daryl Ellis attempted to swim the entire length of Lake Okanagan to raise money for cancer research. As he swam past Rattlesnake Island, he witnessed two creatures twenty to thirty feet in length swimming beneath him for a considerable amount of time, suggesting that there may be an entire population of Ogopogo creatures.

Ogopogo continues to be sighted by numerous witnesses every year, particularly in waters near the city of Kelowna. Its likeness appears on postcards and trinkets, as well as a statue in Kelowna's City Park.

Ol' Slavey

> **CHARACTERISTICS:** Serpentine, with a long neck
>
> **SIZE:** Anywhere from thirty to sixty feet long
>
> **HABITAT:** Great Slave Lake in the Northwest Territories of Canada
>
> **APPETITE:** Fish, hopefully

Named after the Slave tribe of Native Americans, the Great Slave Lake is the deepest body of freshwater in North America, reaching depths of 2,015 feet. The lake is said to be the home of a relatively new lake monster known as Ol' Slavey. An ordained priest named Jim Lynn spotted the creature in September of 2004 near the gold mining town of Yellowknife. Lynn only claimed to see the serpent's neck as it moved through the lake but stated that it appeared to rise at least six feet above the water—which definitely makes you wonder just how large the part of the creature beneath the waves really was.

Old Yellow Top

> **CHARACTERISTICS:** Bigfoot creature with black fur, except for a long tuft of blond fur on the top of its head
>
> **SIZE:** Six to seven feet tall

Old Yellow Top is an individual Sasquatch or Bigfoot creature seen near the town of Cobalt in Ontario, Canada. All accounts of the monster match descriptions of Sasquatch and Bigfoot lore, save one identifying characteristic—the beast has a head of blond hair.

Old Yellow Top—once simply known as "Yellow Top" but later renamed because of its age—was seen by miners and prospectors in the early 1900s. Sightings continued through the century up until the 1970s, when a busload of miners swerved off the road and crashed to avoid hitting the creature.

Ponik

In 1973, the municipality of Pohenegamook was formed from the three villages of Saint Eleuthere, Estcourt and Scully, which share a lake of the same name. Just a year later, during the centennial celebration of Saint Eleuthere, the village named its local lake monster. Ponik, as the creature came to be called, has been seen since around 1874 but without much celebration. The monster began making more of a stir in the late 1950s, when appearances drastically increased during the restoration of Road 289, which runs along the lake. Apparently the dynamiting of the road upset the creature's normal habits, and it surfaced more often than usual.

Like many lake monsters, Ponik is described as serpentine with humps. From its horse-like head protrude catfish-like whiskers, which have led some to compare the creature to the legendary Chinese Dragon.

Pressie

CHARACTERISTICS: Dark serpentine body with a long neck, whale-like tail, and whiskers

SIZE: Approximately seventy-five feet long

HABITAT: Lake Superior

APPETITE: Fish and the occasional deer

PRECAUTIONS: Has been known to attack humans, and uses its snaky body to crush its victims in the same manner as a boa constrictor.

Lake Superior is home to a seldom seen lake monster known as Pressie, which is named for the Presque Isle River—an area where the beast was photographed by a hiker in 1977.

While reports of Pressie are few, they are quite dramatic. In 1897, a yacht struck a rock near Duluth and one man fell overboard. His three horror-stricken shipmates watched as a serpentine beast tried to constrict him in an anaconda-like fashion. Fortunately, the man somehow managed to escape. In the mid-1990s, a group of fishermen reported seeing a wading deer pulled under the water, presumably to be devoured. The only thing left was the deer's severed head.

The Thetis Lake Monster

CHARACTERISTICS: Humanoid with a fish mouth, scales, webbed hands and feet, and cold black eyes

---

SIZE: Approximately five feet tall, weighing around 150 pounds

HABITAT: Thetis Lake, Victoria, British Columbia

APPETITE: Carnivorous

Looking very much like the monster from *Creature From the Black Lagoon*, a fish-man known as the Thetis Lake Monster made quite a stir in the 1970s. The monster first appeared in 1972, when it surprised two teenagers on the beach by launching from the water and attacking them. The pair escaped, but not without one of the young men receiving a cut on his hand from the sharp fin protruding from the monster's head. Other witnesses sighted the creature during the next few days—though those encounters were less dramatic.

Descriptions of the Thetis Lake Monster, with its scaly body and webbed appendages and fins, bear a resemblance to a creature of Native American legend known as the Pugwis. The Kwakiutl tribe of the Puget Sound region told of the monster, which was described as a carnivorous beast-man with a fish-like face.

Waheela

CHARACTERISTICS: A large wolflike animal

SIZE: Three to four feet tall at the shoulder

HABITAT: Alaska and the Northwest Territories of Canada

APPETITE: Carnivore

PRECAUTIONS: According to Inuit legend, the Waheela likes to decapitate its victims.

Also known as "bear-dogs," the Waheela are large canines that inhabit the frozen areas surrounding the Alaska/Canada border. The subject of modern sightings as well as legend, many believe the Waheela to be a type of prehistoric wolf known as a *dire wolf*, or possibly a hyena-like creature similar to another cryptid, the Shunka Warakin. In native legend, the Waheela is a giant supernatural wolf, sometimes referred to as Amarok, which inhabits the Nahanni Valley and removes the heads of its victims.

Wendigo

CHARACTERISTICS: Tall and lanky with sickeningly yellow skin	

CHARACTERISTICS: Tall and lanky with sickeningly yellow skin

SIZE: Ten to fifteen feet tall

HABITAT: Canada and the northern United States

APPETITE: Originally human, Wendigos are cannibalistic

PRECAUTIONS: Wendigos delight in driving humans to the point of insanity just before devouring them.

Although in recent times Wendigo has often been associated with Sasquatch or Bigfoot lore, the monsters actually bear little similarity when you consider the Native American and Inuit legends of the creature. A Wendigo (also known by other similar Native American names such as Windigo, Witigo, or Wiindigoo) is usually regarded as a malevolent spirit of the woods that was originally a human but was transformed by evil magic. In most cases, a person becomes a Wendigo after she becomes lost in the frigid forests of the north and resorts to cannibalism.

Wendigo descriptions vary, but most traditions portray the beast as very tall with yellowed skin, a long bluish tongue and a heart of ice. Wendigo are very thin—almost skeletal—and are usually missing lips and toes, as before the loss of their humanity they likely fell victim to frostbite and starvation.

Wendigo are supernaturally in tune with the forest and nature and use their powers to stalk their prey. The beasts can alter the weather, often creating blinding snowstorms to ensnare their victims. They can move through the forest almost invisibly, toying with their victims before the impending kill. They have the power to inflict a terrible fever upon their intended prey, which causes them to suffer horrible nightmares and intense burning pain in their legs until they are driven mad and tear off all of their clothes to flee insanely into the forest where the Wendigo await them.

According to legend, the only way to kill a Wendigo is to destroy its frozen heart—either by melting it somehow or driving a silver stake into it. Dismemberment of a Wendigo's corpse using a sliver blade is also recommended. In the early 1900s, a Cree shaman named Jack Fiddler claimed to have killed fourteen of the monsters during his lifetime. He and his younger brother Joseph were convicted of murder in 1907 after killing a woman who they claimed was undergoing the Wendigo metamorphosis and was a threat to their entire tribe.

Winnipogo

Winnipogo is a population of lake serpents living in Lake Winnipeg and the surrounding lakes and rivers.

See also *Manipogo,* page 167.

Monsters of
Mexico

MEXICO

El Chupacabra

> **CHARACTERISTICS:** Descriptions vary, but typically gray and gargoyle-like in appearance, with large red eyes
>
> ---
>
> **SIZE:** Three to four feet tall
>
> ---
>
> **HABITAT:** Puerto Rico, Mexico and the United States
>
> ---
>
> **APPETITE:** Drinks the blood of livestock
>
> ---
>
> **PRECAUTIONS:** Incredibly aggressive

"It's not a vampire … and it's not that Mexican goat-sucker either."

—Special Agent Dana Scully,
The X Files

Ask almost anyone and they will probably know what El Chupacabra is. The name is a literal Spanish translation meaning "goat-sucker," and the creature is without a doubt the most talked-about cryptid animal in our culture today. Exposure on the Internet and pop culture references have propelled the creature's notoriety to the forefront of monster-lore. The creature is probably second only to Bigfoot in North American monster fame.

First treated as an urban legend, the story of El Chupacabra began as an explanation for an epidemic of slaughtered livestock in Puerto Rico in the early 1990s. Goats and other livestock were found with small puncture wounds in their necks and completely drained of blood. The story spread, and Chupacabra attacks and sightings began to crop up throughout Mexico and in the southwestern United States.

Descriptions of the creature vary quite a bit and suggest that Chupacabra lore may have been used to explain what may indeed be several different cryptid animals. The animal is usually described in a couple of ways:

- A gray, bipedal lizard-like being with skinny, clawed forearms and strong hind legs that it uses to move with a hopping motion. It has fangs, a forked tongue and a row of sharp quills down its spine. The creature has large eyes with no eyelids. This version of El Chupacabra is often compared to the gray alien of extraterrestrial lore. Many believe the beast to be otherworldly in origin.

- A ferocious kangaroo or wallaby-like animal that has a snout full of ferocious fangs and a long tail. Descriptions of this version vary between having gray fur and being hairless with bluish gray mottled skin. There are many similarities between this description and that of the Phantom Kangaroo or Devil Monkey.

While El Chupacabra is a relatively new monster, the phenomena may not be. A legend from Puerto Rico in the 1970s tells of El Vampiro de Moca, a supposed vampire in the small town of Moca who killed livestock. Some natives of South America tell of a mosquito-man who drinks the blood of animals through its long nose.

The Tecoluta Sea Monster

CHARACTERISTICS: Serpentine, covered in hard platelike armor, with a ten-foot-long tusk protruding from its head section

SIZE: Approximately thirty-five tons

HABITAT: Waters near Tecoluta, Mexico

APPETITE: Unknown

In March of 1969, the remains of a very large creature were found deposited on a beach near Tecoluta, Mexico. The beast was unidentifiable with its jointed body armor and one-ton tusk. While some biologists suggested that the carcass might be that of a narwhal or possibly a finback whale, the discovery drew international interest, and the mayor of Tecoluta allowed the creature to remain unburied as a tourist attraction despite its rotting stench.

More Monsters
of North America

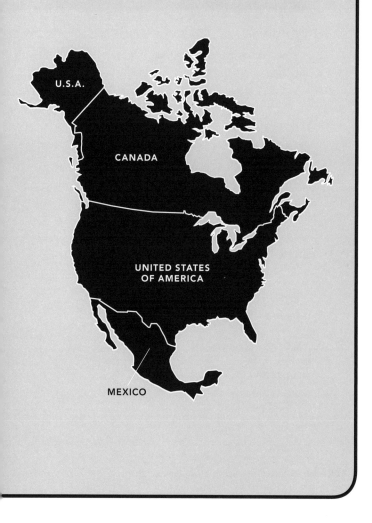

The Argopelter

CHARACTERISTICS: Thought to resemble a monkey or squirrel, though few have ever seen one of these elusive animals

SIZE: Unknown

HABITAT: Forests of the United States

APPETITE: Unknown

PRECAUTIONS: Be careful when walking in the woods, as this creature is fond of throwing sticks and other debris.

While rarely (if ever) seen, this creature of lumberjack folklore is thought to live in the trunks of hollow trees. The Argopelter likes to climb into the high branches and wait for someone to walk beneath it. It then pelts them with sticks, tree bark, fruit and whatever else it can find.

Black Dogs

CHARACTERISTICS: Ghostly black canines with fiery red eyes

SIZE: Varies from typical dog-size to that of a calf

HABITAT: Worldwide

APPETITE: Unknown

Phantom black dogs have been reported in much of the world. With sightings dating back to the 1100s, Great Britain has a rich folklore full of reports of black dogs that haunt desolate roads, churchyards, bridges, crossroads and gateways. In England, the legends are very prevalent—a mysterious black ghost-dog is the basis for the famous Sherlock Holmes story *The Hound of the Baskervilles* by Sir Arthur Conan Doyle.

When settlers arrived in the New World, apparently the legends and curses associated with black dogs followed. Particularly in New England, North America has its own share of black ghost-dogs. They are typically reported in cemeteries but seem to haunt any place that has some sort of supernatural significance. They are thought to be spectral sentries charged with protecting the remains of their former masters or guarding some sort of threshold, such as a cemetery gate.

In many legends, the appearance of a black dog is an omen of ill fate—often death. Strangely enough, black dogs are often reported as seeming friendly and only seem to become aggressive when one gets too close to whatever they may be guarding.

Devil Monkeys

CHARACTERISTICS: Gray fur, powerful hind legs, small forearms, long bushy tail; capable of hopping long distances

SIZE: Three to five feet tall

HABITAT: Worldwide

APPETITE: Carnivorous

PRECAUTIONS: These animals are very aggressive.

Devil Monkeys is the name given by cryptozoologists to a group of creatures that have been sighted all over the United States and in other parts of the world as well. They are described as having baboon-like faces and kangaroo-like bodies. The creatures move by hopping like kangaroos and have been reported to cover as much as seventy-five feet in only a couple of hops.

Devil Monkeys are very fierce animals. They have been known to attack dogs and are not necessarily shy of humans. They sometimes try to claw their way into people's homes, have attacked cars from time to time and have been blamed for the death of livestock on numerous occasions.

See also *Phantom Kangaroos,* page 195; and *The Enfield Horror,* page 92.

Flitterbick

CHARACTERISTICS: Probably much like a flying squirrel in appearance, though a live Flitterbick has never been seen

SIZE: Unspecified

HABITAT: North America

APPETITE: Unknown

The Flitterbick is a folklore animal closely related to the flying squirrel, with one incredible difference. Flitterbicks fly at such high speeds that they are practically invisible. Collision with a Flitterbick is usually fatal. Descriptions of the darting flying movements of the creature are strikingly similar to the mysterious worldwide UFO phenomenon known as Rods.

See also *Rods,* page 196.

Freshwater Octopus

> **CHARACTERISTICS:** Gray in color, resembles saltwater octopus species such as *Octopus burryi*
>
> ---
>
> **SIZE:** Approximately three feet long
>
> ---
>
> **HABITAT:** Rivers in the Midwest and the South
>
> ---
>
> **APPETITE:** Probably fish
>
> ---
>
> **PRECAUTIONS:** Typically shy of humans; no evidence suggests these creatures are particularly harmful

Since the 1950s, there have been reports of octopi showing up in unseemly areas. The creatures have been caught by fishermen in rivers in West Virginia and Kentucky. They've been seen swimming in the Ohio River—a fresh carcass was even found washed up on the river bank. Theories abound about the existence of a freshwater species of octopus. Some scientists speculate that an octopus may venture upstream from native waters during a period of time at the end of its life known as *senescence,* when the octopus basically goes crazy and spends its time wandering aimlessly. Of course, a misplaced octopus could only venture so far into freshwater, and the chance that a saltwater animal could make it as far as the Midwest is unheard of. Many believe the sightings to be simply cases of an animal being cruelly released from its marine aquarium into a freshwater environment where it stands no chance of survival.

Giant Catfish

CHARACTERISTICS: It's a catfish … only really big.

SIZE: Over nine feet in length

APPETITE: Fish and vegetation

PRECAUTIONS: Catfish can be carnivorous. One should regard a catfish of this magnitude as one does a shark.

Reports of giant catfish living in lakes and rivers across the United States may sound like the stuff of urban legend or a wild fishing story. How large are we talking? Let's say approximately ten feet long and weighing about five hundred pounds. A freshwater fish of this size is hard to believe, but is it beyond the realm of possibility? Stories told by divers and welders working on dams in the Ohio and Mississippi Rivers tell of fish of this size. In some cases, workers refuse to go back in the water after seeing the beasts.

While the largest catfish caught in North America is around four feet long and 120 pounds, catfish in parts of Asia can reach nine feet in length and weigh over 600 pounds.

Interestingly, some reports of lake monsters could actually be attributed to giant catfish if such creatures indeed exist. After all, many lake serpents are said to have catfish-like whiskers or beards.

The Hidebehind

CHARACTERISTICS: No description available

SIZE: Unknown

HABITAT: Forests of the United States

APPETITE: Human flesh

PRECAUTIONS: This predatory creature is a known man-eater and moves with incredible speed.

The Hidebehind gets its name for its amazing ability to always be behind its victim. The beast lurks behind tree trunks until it has a chance to get behind an unsuspecting person in the woods. A Hidebehind may be heard, but no matter how quickly one is able to turn around, the monster is always able to move behind them. The creature often uses its speed to toy with victims in this manner before finally dragging them off and devouring them. The Hidebehind has been blamed for the deaths and disappearances of many lumberjacks throughout the years. No one has ever seen one and lived to offer a description.

Phantom Felines

> **CHARACTERISTICS:** Mountain lion or panther-like cats, usually black
> ------
> **SIZE:** Three to four feet tall at the shoulder
> ------
> **HABITAT:** Throughout North America, in areas that such cats do not typically inhabit
> ------
> **APPETITE:** Carnivorous

Large cats are obviously real. But what about reports of strange black panthers lurking around the Midwest or the Appalachian Mountains? Black panthers have been seen all across our continent, though according to mainstream zoology, large black cats do not inhabit North America. These elusive mystery cats display aggressive behavior and have reportedly attacked moving automobiles and have been blamed for the slaughter of livestock.

Phantom Kangaroos

> **CHARACTERISTICS:** Resemble a kangaroo or wallaby, but seem to be more ferocious
> ------
> **SIZE:** Three to five feet tall

HABITAT: Throughout North America, particularly the Midwest and the South

---

APPETITE: Carnivorous

PRECAUTIONS: These animals are incredibly aggressive and capable of hopping at great speeds.

A prime example of an animal turning up where it shouldn't, Phantom Kangaroos have been seen on numerous occasions across the continent—with most reports occurring in the Midwest. In instances of Phantom Kangaroo sightings, the first inclination is to check with local zoos that usually report no animals missing. To make matters stranger, the kangaroos do not appear to be normal. They seem overly aggressive and have fierce teeth.

These creatures have been sighted in rural areas hopping along railroad tracks. They sometimes charge automobiles or try to force their way into homes. Phantom Kangaroos have even been sighted in large cities. During the fall of 1974 in Chicago, a pair of police officers cornered a strange growling marsupial in an alley and exchanged blows with the beast before it escaped.

 ## Rods

CHARACTERISTICS: Cylindrical, with appendages that move in an undulating or spiral motion; they fly through the air at incredible speeds; nearly invisible to the naked eye

SIZE: Ranges from a few inches to several feet

HABITAT: Worldwide

APPETITE: Unknown

Discovered through the use of film and video, the phenomena known as Rods—also referred to as Sky Fish—represent some the most interesting and controversial evidence that exists concerning the subject of UFOs. When almost any video or film is played at slow motion, Rods can be seen zipping through the air intelligently avoiding collision with people and objects.

First discovered in 1994 when filmmaker Jose Escamilla noticed strange cylindrical shapes flying through the frames of a film he shot in Midway, New Mexico, Rods have since been seen in videos around the globe. Many have tried to debunk their existence, claiming

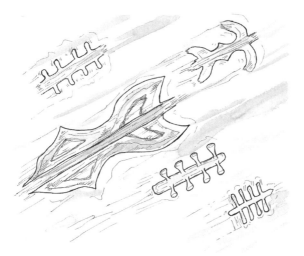

that the shapes are merely tricks of light, or a strange visual effect created by insects caught on camera, but the subject remains one of heated debate between skeptics and believers. UFO investigators who intentionally capture Rods on camera take measures to ensure their lenses are free of dust and obstruction, they use tripods to steady their devices, and they are careful to point out the differences between flying birds and insects and what they believe are true Rods.

If Rods do exist, the big question is what they are. Are these weird cylindrical objects an elusive species of flying animal, or are they visitors from another world?

Skin-walker

> **CHARACTERISTICS:** Human capable of transforming into a predatory creature such as a wolf or coyote
>
> ---
>
> **SIZE:** Varies
>
> ---
>
> **HABITAT:** North America
>
> ---
>
> **APPETITE:** Carnivorous

The term Skin-walker has been used in popular culture to represent a collection of Native American accounts of werewolf-like creatures. Skin-walkers are humans capable of changing into the form of an animal or several animals.

While used liberally to describe various Native American legends, the term Skin-walker comes from

Navajo tradition and describes the legend of the *yee nadlooshii*, a shaman who gained dark supernatural powers after murdering a relative. Aside from the power of shape-shifting, the Skin-walker is said to desecrate anything holy and rob graves in order to gather human remains. It grinds the cadavers into a powder, which it then sprinkles upon victims, cursing them with illness or death.

Snipes

CHARACTERISTICS: Small birds with colored feathers and luminous eyes

---

SIZE: Approximately six inches long

HABITAT: Rural areas of North America

APPETITE: Insects

Snipes tend to live in marshlands, though sometimes they are said to inhabit cornfields, forests or even desolate stretches of road. Snipes are beautiful birds with shimmering feathers of blue and gold, similar to peacock feathers. The birds are nocturnal and have glowing eyes. Because of their spectacular feathers, Snipes are valuable, and people often try to capture them. Typically, people hunt for Snipes in the following manner: A group of friends drives to a desolate location and lets one member of the party out of the car and gives them a sack made of burlap or linen—the rest of the group then drives to a nearby location to flush the Snipes out, running them toward the person left holding the bag.

Snow Snakes

CHARACTERISTICS: Snow-white in color

SIZE: Varies

HABITAT: Northern United States

APPETITE: Rabbits and other small creatures

PRECAUTIONS: Extremely venomous and nearly invisible in the snow.

Unlike other reptiles, Snow Snakes do not hibernate during the winter—in fact, they thrive in the cold. These unique vipers are completely white, giving them the ability to hide in the snow until their unsuspecting prey happens by. The creatures are reported to be highly venomous, and victims usually die within a matter of seconds. The best chance of spotting a snow snake before it's too late is to look for its eyes, which are pink.

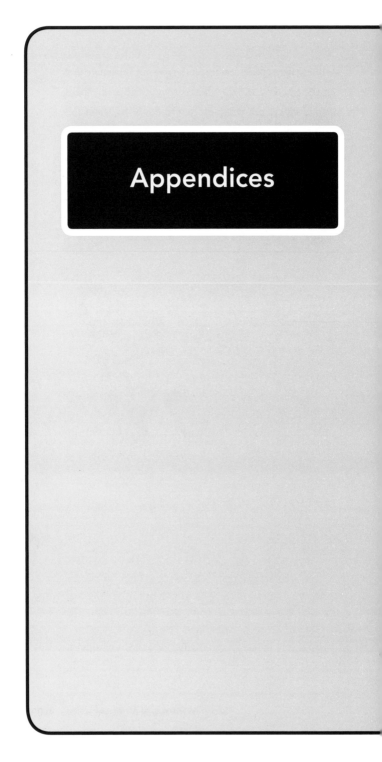

Appendices

APPENDIX A

Remedial Monster School

Welcome to Remedial Monster School. You're here either because you are a complete novice when it comes to monsters, because there are few background things about monsters you need to bone up on or because you simply find my book entertaining (in which case, I like your style).

What follows is some information on well-known monsters that you should have already heard of. We're talking monster movie type stuff… plus a few things you might have seen on the Discovery Channel.

The Usual Suspects

VAMPIRES

"To become a vampire they have to suck your blood. Then you have to suck their blood. It's a whole big sucking thing—mostly they're just going to kill you."

—**Buffy Summers,**
Buffy the Vampire Slayer

Vampires are undead people who feed upon the blood of humans. In modern vampire tales, the creatures mingle their blood with chosen victims to create new vampires. Their feeding is more than a simple need for food and is usually portrayed as a dark sexual act. Vampires feed on blood, yes—but also upon fear and desire. These legendary monsters are incredibly seductive with their promise of immortality and eternal youth. Becoming a vampire has a price, of course. Your soul is damned.

For this reason, vampires cannot venture into the daylight, cannot tread upon sacred ground, cast no reflection and are repelled by the sight of the crucifix. Holy water may be used to burn a vampire—in fact, almost anything blessed, such as communion wafers, can ward off the creature. Vampires are also repelled by garlic and cannot enter a home uninvited.

You can destroy a vampire by driving a wooden stake through its heart. Incineration and decapitation are also effective methods.

A few lesser known tactics:

- Bury a suspected vampire upside down to prevent it from rising.

- Scatter small seeds, such as poppy seeds, around the gravesite of a suspected vampire—when it arises, it will be preoccupied with counting the seeds. You may also fill a suspected vampire's coffin with sawdust for the same reason—in theory the vampire will count the particles each night and be unable to rise.

- A branch of wild rose or hawthorn may repel a vampire.

WEREWOLVES

Werewolves are humans who turn into large wolves or wolflike creatures during the full moon and hunt other humans. Their bloodlust is insatiable. Werewolves kill for both hunger and pleasure.

The ability to transform into a werewolf is known as lycanthropy. Humans become werewolves in a variety of ways. They may seek to become a werewolf of their own volition in order to perform dark deeds—to do so involves sorcery and is typically accomplished by donning an enchanted garment made of wolf skin or by rubbing the naked body with a magical salve. More often, humans become werewolves as the result of a curse—in werewolf form, they kill without wanting to, and in human form, they are forced to endure the knowledge of what they have done as wolves under the thrall of the full moon. Modern werewolf legends tend to suggest that one becomes a werewolf after suffering the bite of another werewolf. In the original legends, however, werewolf attacks rarely left victims alive.

Protection against werewolves usually requires a weapon made of silver—an axe, dagger or silver bullet. The poisonous herb aconitum, commonly known as wolfsbane, is sometimes said to repel werewolves—though in other legends, it is an ingredient used in ointments that induce lycanthropy.

ZOMBIES

Put simply, zombies are dead human beings that have been brought back to life. In most folkloric accounts, zombies are created by a form of dark magic and used as slaves. According to some accounts of voodoo practices, a magician named a bokor reanimates corpses to create zombies that serve him, because as the undead they have no will of their own. There are also accounts where the bokor creates a potion that is ingested by his victim, making her appear lifeless—he returns for her buried "corpse" later and inducts the person into servitude, where she works for him in a drugged state.

Voodoo zombies are a large part of zombie lore. In modern tales, however, zombies can manifest themselves in several different forms, all of which have

subtly different characteristics. Mostly, these zombies are portrayed as flesh-eating cadavers that have risen from the grave. Their bite is infectious and causes the victim to gradually become another zombie. While loosely based on some historical folklore representations of the undead, this portrayal is largely a product of horror movie culture, where the dead are reanimated by interplanetary radiation, military chemical warfare or by extraterrestrials who employ zombies as soldiers in their goal of planetary domination. Real zombies are usually poor mindless slaves who are doomed to labor for a puppet master who robs them of their eternal rest.

To be on the safe side, if you encounter a zombie, it is wise to keep your distance. If it tries to attack you, a sharp blow to the head is considered an effective technique for destroying the zombie. Dismemberment is also an option. If you suspect someone has been bitten by a zombie, you should watch him very closely for signs of infection.

The Big Three of Cryptozoology

Cryptozoology is the study of strange animals that are believed by conventional science to be nonexistent. If you're wondering which monsters are most likely to exist within the realm of scientific possibility, well, here they are. These are the three most-researched monsters in the world. Due to the sheer number of sightings, the credibility of witnesses and the strength of evidence gathered, cryptozoologists tend to lend the most credence to the three monsters that follow:

BIGFOOT

This tall, hairy monster got its name in 1958 when a Northern California newspaper printed an article about a construction worker who collected a plaster cast of a large footprint he had found in the Bluff Creek Valley. Sightings of the monster continued, and Bigfoot gained notoriety. In 1967, the creature was captured on film by Bigfoot enthusiasts Roger Patterson and Bob Gimlin—an event that launched Bigfoot to the forefront of monster stardom. See *Bigfoot,* page 146.

Incidentally, the term "Bigfoot" occurs in this book eighty times.

THE ABOMINABLE SNOWMAN

Also known as Yeti, this hairy ape-man is one of the longest reported unproven creatures known to man. Reportedly living in the Himalayan mountains, the Abominable Snowman has much in common with western Bigfoot lore. Its footprints are approximately three times as large as those of a normal human.

THE LOCH NESS MONSTER

Like I said in the beginning of this book, it's hard to write a book about monsters and not talk about Nessie. This famous monster of Scotland's Loch Ness became world renowned in 1933, after roughly twenty sightings occurred over the span of six months. The frequency of the sightings was most likely due to construction work on an old road running along the lake. The use of dynamite most likely disturbed the creature, causing it to show itself. Since then, reports of Nessie have continued, and the monster has been the subject of much research and controversy. Photographs and film footage of an unidentified creature both on the surface and underwater exist. From studying these photos, many have come to the conclusion that Nessie is a prehistoric reptile known as a plesiosaur or an extinct whale known as a Zeuglodon.

Monster Spotter's Tool Kit

The successful monster spotter is a prepared monster spotter. When doing research or conducting an investigation of a monster sighting or simply exploring an area of reported paranormal activity, it is important to have the necessary equipment on hand.

The bare essentials:

- Flashlight
- Notebook
- Pencil or pen

With these three items, you can begin a basic investigation. It's always good practice to have a flashlight on hand. A pocket notebook and a writing implement will allow you to jot down details that you may forget later. I recommend having these items with you at all times, as you never know when you might stumble upon a clue that can aid you in your forays into monster spotting—for example, you might be simply enjoying a frothy refreshment at your favorite establishment and meet someone who has a monster story to tell (it's good practice to steer conversations with strangers toward the paranormal … it's a great way to make friends and a sure path toward instant popularity).

Getting Down to Business

Of course, for some serious monster spotting, you'll need more—you'll need equipment for gathering evidence to support your wild claims. Plus, your adventure may take you into small towns, the wilderness or maybe a sewer. I suggest carrying a backpack with the following:

- Handheld tape recorder (preferably one with an automatic voice-activation setting)
- Digital camera
- Cellular telephone
- Swiss Army-style pocket knife or utility tool
- Duct tape
- First aid kit
- Area maps
- Compass
- Field glasses
- Plaster of Paris
- Bottled water or canteen
- Food rations
- Sunscreen
- Insect repellent
- Zagat Restaurant Survey

OTHER EQUIPMENT

- Video camera
- 35mm camera (Traditional film may prove easier to authenticate. Digital photos are easily manipulated, and some sad little skeptic with little happiness in his life may feel the need to insinuate that your evidence is a hoax in order to destroy your credibility and make himself feel like a big person, which makes him no better than a schoolyard bully.)

EQUIPMENT NOT ENDORSED BY *THE MONSTER SPOTTER'S GUIDE TO NORTH AMERICA*

Should you feel compelled to carry any of the following items, neither the author of this book nor the publisher will accept any responsibility for any resulting incidents.

- Firearms
- Explosives
- Tranquilizer guns
- Steel traps
- Harpoons
- Wooden stakes
- Silver bullets
- Pitchforks
- Flaming torches

APPENDIX C

Monster Spotter's Glossary

ALIEN - In paranormal research, the term alien is often used to describe a visitor from outer space. Popular culture has made it easy to associate the word with the typical space man depiction: gray body with spindly limbs, a bulbous head and large dark eyes. Space aliens have been reported with other appearances as well. There are tall, reptilian, praying mantis-like creatures and giant fair-haired humanoids. All reportedly travel in flying saucers.

BIPED - An animal that walks on two legs.

BUNYIP - A legendary aboriginal creature reported to inhabit lakes and rivers in Australia. Bunyips are often considered as supporting testimony to the possible existence of lake monsters.

COELACANTH - A prehistoric fish thought to be extinct but rediscovered in the late 1930s off the coast of Southern Africa. The coelacanth has been a boon for cryptozoology, offering tangible evidence that species can reemerge after surviving undetected throughout the ages. Because such a fish exists, it gives hope that other species might be discovered or rediscovered.

CRYPTID - An animal species that is not believed to exist by traditional science. Cryptids can be prehistoric creatures thought to be extinct that reemerge, or creatures that have yet to be discovered.

CRYPTOZOOLOGIST - A researcher who searches for and studies evidence suggesting the existence of animals believed nonexistent by mainstream science.

CRYPTOZOOLOGY - A fringe science dedicated to the study of animals whose reported existence is unproven.

DRACONTOLOGY - Literally, this term means the study of dragons, though it is also widely used by cryptozoologists to refer to research on serpentine lake monsters.

EXTRATERRESTRIAL - Most widely used as a more accurate term applied to what people typically call aliens or space aliens. While alien may mean anything foreign, the term extraterrestrial means "not of the Earth" and may be used as an adjective to describe anything that could originate from outer space (a meteor, for example). The term is most often used as a noun meaning "a being from outer space."

FORTEAN - A term applied to paranormal phenomena. Named after Charles Fort (1874–1932), whose forays into the paranomal included investigations of ghosts, lake monsters, UFOs, strange lights and a range of unexplained events and manifestations. Fort's work inspired many researchers, and there have been several associations named after him as well as the *Fortean Times*, a widely known journal of paranormal studies.

GLOBSTER - A beached carcass of an alleged sea monster or lake serpent. The term may also refer to monster remains found inside the belly of another creature such as a shark or killer whale.

GREYS - A term widely used to describe the most prevalent description of extraterrestrial life forms. Greys are named for the color of their skin and have large bulbous heads and large, oval-shaped dark eyes. Their mouths are small with no lips, and their noses are little more than two tiny slits in their flat faces. They typically lack ears and are believed to communicate through telepathy. Greys have come to dominate space alien lore and have all but phased out the "little green men" alien archetype of yesteryear. The motives of greys are the subject of wide speculation—they are often portrayed as sinister beings who abduct humans to conduct experiments upon them, though some believe them to be benevolent misunderstood beings seeking to commune with humanity.

HOMINID - A member of the scientific family of large apes, or hominidae, such as a gorilla or chimpanzee. There is wide speculation that many hairy monsters such as Bigfoot are actually undiscovered species of hominids.

HOMINOLOGY - A term widely used in Bigfoot/Sasquatch research that refers to the study of the connection between humans and primates.

HUMANOID - Having a humanlike form or stature, or other human characteristics.

LIVING FOSSIL - A living specimen from a group of organisms thought to be extinct.

LYCANTHROPE - A human who possesses the ability to transform into a wolf either by choice or because of a curse. More commonly known as a werewolf.

MEN IN BLACK - UFO culture often speaks of mysterious nondescript men dressed in black attire who interrogate and often terrorize eyewitnesses. These men ask odd questions, offer strange credentials and sometimes threaten people who might disclose their UFO experiences to the media. There has been much speculation on the identities of Men in Black. Some believe they are agents of a secret government organization in charge of covering up the truth and spreading disinformation about UFO phenomena. Others believe they are extraterrestrials themselves.

NAPE - A term coined by noted cryptozoologist Loren Coleman to label apelike animals reported throughout North America. The term was created by blending words from the phrase North American Ape.

PARANORMAL - A word used to describe an occurrence or observation that defies scientific explanation.

PLESIOSAUR - An aquatic prehistoric reptile with small head, long neck, flippers, and a body that is somewhat like a turtle with no shell. Many believe that a few individuals from this species of dinosaurs may have survived and are responsible for sightings of lake and sea monsters such as the Loch Ness Monster, Ogopogo and Champ.

TRICKSTER - A supernatural figure appearing in the folklore and mythology of many tribes of indigenous peoples. A trickster may assume different guises and tends to play mischief, often with a fortuitous outcome.

UFOLOGIST - A person who studies UFO-related phenomena.

UFOLOGY - The study of the phenomena of unidentified flying objects, or UFOs.

URBAN LEGEND - An unsubstantiated modern folk tale of horror or fantastic events spread by word of mouth or by related means. Well-known urban legends include accounts of alligators living in the sewers of New York City, a ghost known as Bloody Mary who appears in your bathroom mirror if you say her name three times and a murderous man with a hook for a hand who attacks amorous youths engaged in the act of "parking."

YETI - While the West has widely referred to this monster as the Abominable Snowman, Yeti is the preferred term. This intelligent ape-man of the Himalayas is one of the most well-known monsters in the world. The Yeti is a giant hairy creature with large humanoid feet.

ZEUGLODON - A serpent-like prehistoric whale of gigantic proportions (fifty to seventy-five feet in length) that has been the subject of many theories to explain reports of sea serpents and lake monsters. Sometimes referred to as Basilosaurus.

APPENDIX D

Monstrous Carcasses

Did you ever say to yourself, "If monsters exist, then how come nobody ever finds a dead one?" Actually, it does happen, smartypants. The most interesting and controversial evidence for the existence of monsters are carcasses. These carcasses may wash up on beaches or are found on the sides of roads. The findings are always the subject of debate, usually due to the condition in which the remains are found. Skeptics claim that the dead creatures are unidentifiable because their remains are simply … well, unidentifiable. The corpses are usually bloated and rotting or have suffered considerable damage as a result of the creature's demise. Here are a few of the most famous cases.

DeRidder Roadkill

CHARACTERISTICS: Bushy brown-black fur with primate-like features

SIZE: Comparable to a large dog, such as a Saint Bernard

HABITAT: DeRidder, Louisiana

In 1996, a woman named Barbara Mullins stopped her car on a lonely stretch of road near DeRidder, Louisiana to get a closer look at a strange looking animal carcass on the shoulder of the road. The creature seemed large for a dog and had features that seemed more like those of a primate than a canine. Mullins snapped a few photos that have since been widely circulated on the Internet and have caused quite a stir in the cryptozoological community.

The photos show the remains of a beast that appears to have a baboon-like face and is quite large. Speculation has been made as to the identity of the creature—theories range from El Chupacabra and Devil Monkey to a werewolf of Cajun folklore known as Loup-Garou. Skeptics contend that the photos simply depict the demise of an unfortunate Pomeranian.

See also *El Chupacabra*, page 183; *Devil Monkeys*, page 190; and *Loup-Garou*, page 66.

The Elmendorf Carcass

CHARACTERISTICS: Short, bluish-grey doglike creature with a mottled appearance and a toothy overbite

> **SIZE:** Two to three feet long, weighing approximately twenty pounds
>
> ---
>
> **HABITAT:** Southern Texas

A couple of specimens of Texas's Elmendorf Creature have been acquired. The beasts were discovered attacking chickens and shot by ranchers. These strange hairless canines are thought to be possible evidence of the legendary Chupacabra. DNA testing has provided no conclusive evidence as to the identity of these creatures.

See also *The Elmendorf Creature,* page 124.

The Minnesota Iceman

> **CHARACTERISTICS:** Hairy humanoid corpse frozen in a block of ice in a refrigerated glass coffin
>
> ---
>
> **SIZE:** Approximately six feet tall—ice block is 6' 11" long, 2' 8" wide and 3' 6" deep

This mysterious Sasquatch-like creature was discovered touring the country as an attraction in a traveling sideshow during the 1960s by a college zoology major. The specimen was subjected to detailed study by well-known cryptozoologists Ivan Sanderson and Bernard Heuvelmans over the course of three days before disappearing. The pair found the corpse to be very convincing and collected a large amount of detailed information that helped distinguish the original Iceman from later fakes that began to circulate after its disappearance.

See also *The Minnesota Iceman,* page 101.

 ## Globsters

The term Globster refers to a carcass of an alleged aquatic monster found washed up on a beach or possibly pulled from the stomach of a predator such as a shark.

SOME FAMOUS GLOBSTERS:

CADDY - In 1937, a partially digested Cadborosaurus carcass was found in a stomach of a sperm whale. See *Cadborosaurus,* page 162.

THE EFFINGHAM CARCASS - A strange forty-foot long serpentine creature discovered on Vancouver Island in 1947.

THE MANN HILL BEACH CARCASS - Twenty feet long and weighing two tons, a plesiosaur-like corpse that washed up on a Massachusetts beach in 1970.

THE ST. AUGUSTINE OCTOPUS - A gigantic octopus measuring twenty-three feet in length that was discovered on the beach of Anastasia Island offshore from St. Augustine, Florida, in 1896.

THE SANTA CRUZ SEA MONSTER - In 1925, a carcass resembling a plesiosaur washed up on Moore's

Beach. The beast had a twenty-foot long neck and a thirty-foot long body with a tail.

THE TECOLUTA SEA MONSTER - The body of an unidentifiable serpentine creature with bony, armor-like plates was found on a beach in Tecoluta, Mexico, in 1969. It sported a ten-foot tusk from its head.

APPENDIX E

Monster Time Line

1800s

1800 - Naval hero Stephen Decatur fires cannon at a Jersey Devil spotted over Hanover Iron Works.

1817 - (August) Approximately one hundred sightings of the Gloucester Sea Serpent are reported.

1870 - P.T. Barnum offers fifty thousand dollars for Champ's carcass.

1874 - Charles Fort is born.

1896 - Giant octopus carcass is found on a beach in St. Augustine, Florida.

1898 - Oscar Fulk claims a giant turtle lives in his lake. The Beast of Busco legend is born.

1900s

1909 - (January) Over one thousand Jersey Devil sightings are reported.

1920s

1920 - The term Sasquatch is invented by J.W. Burns.

1924 - Ape Canyon incident—several miners are attacked after firing upon a Sasquatch.

1925 - Sea monster washes up on Moore's Beach near Santa Cruz, California.

1930s

1932 - Charles Fort dies.
- Attempts are made to capture Hodgee using a steel cage and live sea lions.

1933 - Loch Ness Monster sightings begin.
- Cadborosaurus name is selected by newspaper contest.

1937 - Caddy corpse is found in the stomach of a sperm whale.

1940s

1947 - Sea monster carcass is found on a beach near Effingham on Vancouver Island.

1950s

1952 - (Sept. 12) Flatwoods Monster sightings are reported in Braxton County, West Virginia.

1955 - (August 21) Hopkinsville Goblins attack the Sutton family of Kelly, West Virginia.
- (March) First Loveland Frogman sighting reported.

1958 - The name Bigfoot is invented when a Bluff Creek Valley area construction worker unveils a plaster cast of the monster's footprint.

1959 - The term cryptozoology is invented.
- Orange Eyes of Mansfield, Ohio, makes its first appearance.

1960s

1966 - The term Nape is invented by cryptozoologist Loren Coleman.

1967 - The Minnesota Ice Man is studied by cryptozoologists Sanderson and Heuvelmans.
- (October) The infamous Patterson-Gimlin film of Bigfoot is shot.

1969 - The Lake Worth Monster terrorizes Fort Worth, Texas.
- A sea monster is found on the beach in Tecoluta, Mexico.

1970s

1970 - A sea monster is found on Mann Hill Beach in Massachusetts.

- The Farmer City Monster is reported.

1972 - The cult film *The Legend of Boggy Creek*, portraying the Fouke Monster, is released.
- Police officers encounter a Loveland Frogman on two separate occasions.
- (May) Over two hundred sightings of the Cole Hollow Road Monster are reported.
- (July) A rash of Momo sightings begins.

1973 - Reports of a New Jersey Lizard Man circulate.
- The Arkansas State Legislature creates a refuge for river monster Whitey.
- The Enfield Horror is first sighted in Illinois.
- The Murphysboro Mud Monster is sighted in Illinois.

1974 - The first documented Honey Island Swamp Monster sighting occurs.

1977 - (April) The Dover Demon is sighted in Dover, Massachusetts.
- (July 5) Sandra Mansi takes her infamous photograph of Champ.
- (July) A ten-year-old boy is attacked by Thunderbirds in Lawndale, Illinois.
- The Hawley Him is sighted in eastern Texas.

1980s

1982 - Legislation is passed making it unlawful to harm Champ.

1988 - South Carolina Lizard Man attacks are reported in Bishopville, South Carolina.

1990s

1994 - Rods are discovered in film footage.

1995 - The name El Chupacabra surfaces during an epidemic of slaughtered livestock in Puerto Rico.

1996 - DeRidder Roadkill photos are taken.

2000s

2000 - Cancer survivor Daryl Ellis attempts to swim Lake Okanagan and sees Ogopogo.

2004 - (August) The Elmendorf Creature is shot by a Texas rancher.

Resources

Books

Blackman, W. Haden. *The Field Guide to North American Monsters*. New York: Three Rivers Press/Crown Publishers, Inc., 1998.

Bord, Colin and Janet. *Alien Animals*. Harrisburg, PA: Stackpole Books, 1981.

Coleman, Loren. *Mysterious America: The Revised Edition*. New York: Paraview Press, 2004.

Coleman, Loren and Jerome Clark. *Cryptozoology A to Z*. New York: Fireside Books/Simon & Schuster, 1999.

Coleman, Loren and Patrick Huyghe. *The Field Guide to Bigfoot and Other Mystery Primates*. New York: Anomalist Books, 2006.

Coleman, Loren and Patrick Huyghe. *The Field Guide to Lake Monsters, Sea Serpents, and Other Mystery Denizens of the Deep*. New York: Tarcher/Penguin Group, 2003.

Eberhart, George. *Mysterious Creatures: A Guide to Cryptozoology*. Santa Barbara, CA: ABC-CLIO Inc., 2002.

Keel, John A. *The Mothman Prophecies*. Avondale Estates, GA: IllumiNet Press, 1991.

Keel, John A. *Our Haunted Planet*. Lakeville, MN: Galde Press, 2002.

Rose, Carol. *Giants, Monsters & Dragons*. Santa Barbara, CA: ABC-CLIO Inc., 2000.

Web Sites

www.americanmonsters.com

This hip site is a very cool place to start your monster research. It's got tons of info, fun graphics, video clips, interviews and all kinds of other stuff.

www.bigfootencounters.com

Great site for Bigfoot legends and sightings—includes "classic" Bigfoot stories, a list of California sightings, book & film reviews, interviews and more.

www.cryptomundo.com

This forum for serious cryptozoology enthusiasts features postings from some of the most respected leaders in the field—a great place to find (and share) the latest news about elusive animals.

www.cryptozoology.com

Cryptid profiles, books, articles, sightings, chat forum.

www.lorencoleman.com

One of the world's most respected cryptozoologists, Loren Coleman has been conducting field research and writing books on the subject of mystery animals since the 1960s. This site is dedicated to his work and also shares breaking news in the cryptozoology community.

www.newanimal.org

Titled "The Cryptid Zoo: A Menagerie of Cryptozoology," this site is essentially an A-Z listing of cryptid animals and provides an encyclopedic account of their legends and sightings.

www.roadsideamerica.com

Before starting out on a road trip, check this site for listings by state of roadside attractions—you'll find everything from the mysterious to the hilarious.

www.theshadowlands.net

While looking a little like a site for Dungeons & Dragons enthusiasts, this site has lots of great info about lake and sea monsters, mysterious creatures, UFOs and hauntings.

www.sommerland.org

These folks really like dragons. The "dragon existence" page includes listings for some dragon-esque lake monsters.

www.unmuseum.org

The Museum of Unnatural Mystery. The site name pretty much says it all. "Exhibit halls" feature UFOs, cryptozoology, and lots of other weird stuff.

www.weirdus.com

A promotional tool for the *Weird U.S.* series of books, this site has a cool map feature where you click on a state to read about weird stories including hauntings, mysteries, and local legends. The books are fun too.

www.wikipedia.org

During the writing of this book, someone said to me, "Scott, do you believe everything that you read on Wikipedia?" I said "yes."

Case Studies

CASE STUDY NO. 1

The Severed Monster Head

During the research of this book, I was approached by a couple who claimed to have photographic evidence of a real monster. The couple, whom I will simply refer to as the "Masons," wish to remain anonymous in order to avoid possible public ridicule and—in their own words—"those damn paparazzi." Their story goes something like this:

Paul and Rebecca Mason had planned a long weekend trip to Kentucky to visit Paul's parents. Rebecca always enjoys visits with her in-laws because Paul's father is quite a well-spoken conversationalist and knows some very interesting characters. In fact, he had promised to introduce Paul and Rebecca to his newest friend—we'll call him "Buddy"—who happens to be the owner of an area attraction.

Buddy owns a pay-lake, where he charges folks a nominal fee to fish for some of the largest catfish money can buy. The property is fenced in by a painted gate adorned with sun-bleached bones—presumably from cattle. A makeshift Jolly Roger constructed

Photo courtesy of Rebecca "Mason."

from crossed femurs and a painted cartoon skull watch over the entrance, welcoming all who enter the gates. Chickens run freely around the muddy lot and accost visitors, hoping for a handful of corn. The lake itself is a large pond that Buddy restocks when needed. The catfish are fed daily and can grow to be enormous, as evidenced from the scores of yellowing photographs pinned to the cork bulletin board on Buddy's screened-in front porch/business office.

The day of the Mason family's visit, Buddy gave them the grand tour. They strolled around the lake, visited the chicken coop and perused photographs of happy fishermen showing off their prized catfish. Everyone was enjoying themselves, and Buddy decided to move the party inside for some refreshments and a look at a koi aquarium. That's when things took a strange turn. Rebecca had only taken a few steps in the door when she spied something that commanded her full attention. Amid the stacks of magazines, framed newspaper clippings and fishing trophies a strange shape was fixed to the wall. It was obviously a stuffed and mounted head, but the animal defied identification. The head was a little larger of that of a human with no apparent ears and covered in short, shaggy fur. The small mouth was opened, revealing short fang-like canines.

"What the heck … " Rebecca gasped. Paul caught her stare and quickly found himself equally enthralled by the creature's gruesome visage. "Hey man, what is that thing?" he said almost too quickly.

Buddy turned and shrugged. "Oh that?" he said, "My old daddy shot that thing in the woods out back a few years ago. A bunch of people came and took hair samples, but nobody could ever tell us what it is. Some people call it a Sasquatch. Others say it's a Wampus Cat."

Buddy invited Paul to touch the trophy head. Paul claims that the head had a substantial weight and underneath the fur, he could feel the shape of humanlike ears—a detail that would likely be missing from a simple fake.

Photographs of the creature were permitted and are reproduced here for your own speculation. The actual location of Buddy's pay-lake and the names of the parties involved in this story cannot be disclosed in order to protect their privacy.

Photo courtesy of Rebecca "Mason."

CASE STUDY NO. 2

The Lake Leelanau Monster

Vacations often offer excellent opportunities for amateur monster spotters. Whenever on vacation, I recommend investigating the local legends and area folklore. Small local libraries or tourist museums are often good places to start. While your traveling companion inspects handwoven baskets and other crafts made by early settlers, you can usually stumble across an interesting Native American legend that might give you a lead on some monster lore, or you can ask a local historian about monsters and usually get a colorful answer.

During the course of this writing, I went on a vacation with my wife and in-laws to the Grand Traverse Bay area of Michigan. My research had already given me a lead on a monster sighting from the area, and it seemed like the perfect opportunity for further investigation.

The Lake Leelanau Monster is a pretty obscure monster tale. The story revolves around an area of the lake created when a dam was built in the late 1800s. Apparently, the building of the dam changed the shape of Lake Leelanau a little bit. A few new outlets were created where the water rose and submerged trees. According to my research, in 1910, a monster was discovered by a young man fishing in one of these outlets who attempted to tie his boat up to a branch of an underwater tree, which opened its eyes and revealed itself as a monster. Judging from the expression on the museum steward's face when I recounted the tale, she had never heard of the legend.

The Leelanau Historical Museum is a quaint museum/gift shop run by the Leelanau Historical Society and is located right beside a local library in downtown Leland, Michigan. It seemed like the perfect place to begin my investigation. The museum showcases history and artifacts about the diverse culture of the Leelanau Peninsula and surrounding islands. You'll find

Author surveys the water's edge at an outlet of Lake Leelanau. Photo courtesy of Heather Francis.

information about the area fishing industry, the history of Fish Town—a picturesque village where you can catch ferries to nearby North and South Manitou Islands—and a glimpse into the Native American culture of the area.

The staff was quite friendly, despite the fact that I had obviously interrupted their lunch. While my wife quickly found some interesting artifacts to look at in a far corner of the museum, I got down to business.

ME: I'm interested in any legends of monsters from folklore. I found a reported sighting of a monster in Lake Leelanau on the Internet.

MUSEUM STEWARD: Monsters? [smiles and sighs] Well, I guess pretty much any of your larger lakes like Leelanau or Glen Lake… somebody sometime is gonna say they've seen a monster.

ME: It's supposed to look like a stick with eyes.

MUSEUM STEWARD: I've never heard of anything described like that.

ME: Do you know anything about a sawmill in the area? It was supposedly sighted somewhere near there.

She showed me a map and kindly explained a little about the dam and the sawmill and the resulting changes to the lake's shoreline. I thanked her for her time and proceeded to check out the rest of the museum. She later caught me staring at some Native

Investigating a suspicious character. Photo courtesy of Heather Francis.

American art depicting a local Thunderbird legend. In this particular legend, the Thunderbird is known as Animke, a giant bird that created lighting and thunder by flapping its wings. Many Native American myths tell of the Thunderbird working in tandem with other forces to create weather, and in this legend Animke has a counterpart known as Mishii Bizhou, described as lion of the water that could create large waves with its tail. "I was thinking I might find you looking at that," she said. "I started to tell you about them but decided against it. It's really something very different, you know. Those are very spiritual legends. We can't possibly fully understand them because we are strangers to that culture."

It sounded like it might be time to move on to the next phase of my investigation. Armed with some additional information about the area, my wife and I decided to take a leisurely drive around scenic Lake Leelanau ... it was our vacation after all. We found a few interesting things: a swampy looking outlet of the lake near where the original sightings were described, a bowl of delicious white fish chowder at a local restaurant known as the Bluebird, a crazy looking old silo decorated as the tower of Rapunzel, and a very suspicious looking log. Did we ever find the monster? Well ... that's not really the point of Monster Spotting. It's really about enjoying the search.

Whitefish chowder at the Bluebird. Photo courtesy of the author.

Index